PRAISE FOR *IMPLEMENTING SOCIAL-EMOTIONAL LEARNING*

In this important and timely book, Dr. Berman moves from theory to practice regarding social and emotional learning. Offering compelling evidence and vivid case studies, he guides the reader through practical steps for implementing SEL. Teachers and education leaders, policymakers, and parents will find the practical guidance they need to support students' development and promote positive interactions with others.

—Douglas Reeves, CEO, Creative Leadership Solutions; author of *Fearless Schools*

The case studies here closely align with our work on teacher-student relationships. The districts' challenges are presented sensitively, and the cases collectively illustrate the different forms, capacities, and pacing that any approach to school change may require. The "why-what-how" chapters feature some of the best integrations of scientific and practical knowledge I've seen relative to social-emotional learning. The "lessons learned" chapter is spot-on, and the book is a gift to the field as we strive to support positive social-emotional interactions in the classroom and in the broader community.

—Robert C. Pianta, the Batten Bicentennial Professor of Early Childhood Education, School of Education and Human Development, University of Virginia

The pandemic was a vivid reminder of educators' irreplaceable role in promoting students' well-being. Still, that is easier said than done. Implementing Social-Emotional Learning *rises to meet the need. Brimming cover to cover with varied and doable strategies for transforming entire school systems, this book's rich and granular descriptions of six districts amid change show us how talented and committed educators are leading the way. Practical yet inspirational, this book will be devoured, studied, and embraced by those who care about our young people and our schools—and by those who are willing to dig in now to safeguard and enrich their future.*

—Dennis Shirley, the Gabelli Family Faculty Fellow and Professor, Lynch School of Education and Human Development, Boston College; author of *Well-Being in Schools*

This brilliant, easy-to-read book offers insights on the what, the why, and the how of systemic SEL. One particularly unique aspect is that it shows how SEL plays out differently depending upon the students' ages. This book will become a "go to" text for school leaders and will also lead to rich discussions in universities' school of education courses.

—Sara E. Rimm-Kaufman, Commonwealth Professor of Education, University of Virginia

As Sheldon Berman makes clear in his in-depth analysis of SEL implementation in six districts—large and small, rural and suburban—achieving the intended outcomes requires that school leaders make SEL an explicit mission. Everyone who is working to transform schools to support the whole child will benefit from Berman's insights into these six districts' stumbles and triumphs.

—Linda Darling-Hammond, Charles E. Ducommun Professor of Education Emeritus, Stanford University; past Co-Chair of the National Commission on Social, Emotional, and Academic Development

Sheldon Berman shows there is no single approach to implementing social and emotional learning (SEL). His book is a clarion call for a nationwide focus on social, emotional, and academic learning.

—Aaliyah A. Samuel, President and CEO, Collaborative for Academic, Social, and Emotional Learning; Deputy Assistant Secretary, U.S. Department of Education

As our society grapples with deep divisions, school district leaders must commit to action plans that ensure all students are in caring communities that help them thrive. Berman reminds us that the achievements of students and educators emerge from an environment that brings out their best. This book shows leaders how implementing SEL can foster just such an ecosystem for learning.

—Joshua P. Starr, Managing Partner at the International Center for Leadership in Education; former superintendent and former CEO of Phi Delta Kappa International

Implementing Social-Emotional Learning

Insights from School Districts' Successes and Setbacks

Sheldon H. Berman

ROWMAN & LITTLEFIELD
Lanham • Boulder • New York • London

Published by Rowman & Littlefield
An imprint of The Rowman & Littlefield Publishing Group, Inc.
4501 Forbes Boulevard, Suite 200, Lanham, Maryland 20706
www.rowman.com

86-90 Paul Street, London EC2A 4NE

Published in cooperation with The School Superintendents Association

Copyright © 2023 by Sheldon H. Berman

All rights reserved. No part of this book may be reproduced in any form or by any electronic or mechanical means, including information storage and retrieval systems, without written permission from the publisher, except by a reviewer who may quote passages in a review.

British Library Cataloguing in Publication Information Available

Library of Congress Cataloging-in-Publication Data

Names: Berman, Sheldon, 1949- author.
 Title: Implementing social-emotional learning : insights from school districts' successes and setbacks
  / Sheldon H. Berman.
 Description: Lanham, Maryland : Rowman & Littlefield Publishers, 2023. | Includes bibliographical references. | Summary: "This book is a story about promoting systemic change of SEL in the mindset and capabilities of staff, in the structure of the district, and in the vision, mission, and policies that guide the district"-- Provided by publisher.
 Identifiers: LCCN 2023010068 (print) | LCCN 2023010069 (ebook) | ISBN 9781475869330 (cloth) | ISBN 9781475869347 (paperback) | ISBN 9781475869354 (ebook)
 Subjects: LCSH: Affective education--United States. | Affective education--United States--Case studies. | School districts--United States--Administration. | School districts--United States--Administration--Case studies.
 Classification: LCC LB1072 .B56 2023 (print) | LCC LB1072 (ebook) | DDC 370.15/34--dc23/eng/20230324
 LC record available at https://lccn.loc.gov/2023010068
 LC ebook record available at https://lccn.loc.gov/2023010069

*Dedicated to the memory of Eric Schaps (1942–2021):
educator, researcher, organizational leader, visionary;
influential colleague, valued friend,
lifelong student, reflective mentor;
believer in the vision of a peaceful world;
who understood that when care and community
are central to the culture of classrooms and schools,
young people are enabled to grow and thrive
socially, emotionally, and academically.*

Contents

Foreword *Jon Saphier*	ix
Preface	xiii
Chapter 1: Why Does SEL Matter?	1
Chapter 2: What Is SEL?	11
Chapter 3: How Should We Implement SEL?	25
Chapter 4: Striving for Deep and Transformational Learning: Virginia Beach City Public Schools (Virginia)	37
Chapter 5: Responding to Demographic Challenges: Marshalltown Community School District (Iowa)	55
Chapter 6: First Steps: Moriarty–Edgewood School District (New Mexico)	67
Chapter 7: Targeting SEL Standards: Naperville Community Unit School District 203 (Illinois)	75
Chapter 8: Making SEL Foundational: Corvallis School District (Oregon)	91
Chapter 9: Building for Sustainability: Cleveland Metropolitan School District (Ohio)	113
Chapter 10: Promising Practices at the Secondary Level	137

Chapter 11: What Have We Learned? 145

References 167

About the Author 177

Foreword

Jon Saphier

Chances are, you would not be perusing this book if you didn't already believe that youngsters who develop strong social-emotional skills learn more in school and, in fact, do better in life according to such measures of success as earnings, social status, and happiness. The predictive power of IQ scores pales by comparison. So there is little doubt that social-emotional learning (SEL) is worth our attention.

But how do we make our schools reliable engines for teaching children these skills? That is the gap this book addresses. As multiple chapters make clear, buying a curricular SEL program is not enough—in fact, it may not even be the best way to start.

As educators, we manage the social and emotional environments in which our students live. It is not something we can avoid; we either do it consciously and deliberately or unconsciously and without intention, but those environments are always exerting powerful forces on students' capacity to learn. This is because their beliefs about themselves and their relationships with others bear heavily on the energy they can apply to academics.

No one is better qualified to teach us about how to implement social-emotional learning in a comprehensive and sustainable manner than this book's author, Sheldon (Shelley) Berman. Building and nurturing children's social and emotional development has always been his guiding commitment—even before it was called SEL—and I have watched him tackle this important work over the course of four decades.

As a high school social studies teacher, he integrated empathy and perspective-taking into his courses. As the cofounder of Educators for Social Responsibility (now called Engaging Schools), he built a program and an organization that brought SEL to educators throughout the country. The four school districts he led in three states ranged from small to large, and from suburban to urban, and all of them incorporated SEL into their curriculum. The case studies in this book reflect the accumulated wisdom of his hands-on professional history and his continuous study of sustainable SEL implementation.

Shelley's lifelong accomplishments have been recognized repeatedly at the state, national, and international levels. In 2020, on the basis of his district leadership in effective implementation of SEL, he received the Mary Utne O'Brien Award for Excellence in Expanding the Evidence-Based Practice of Social-Emotional Learning. This award is particularly noteworthy because it was presented by the Collaborative for Academic, Social, and Emotional Learning (CASEL). The CASEL organization has been a unifier of the SEL movement since its founding in 1994 and has gathered fifteen years of evidence on the positive effects of SEL work.

However, data and evidence alone rarely lead to a change in behavior. As social creatures, we tend to be more influenced by what our family members, friends, and associates do. That is a point worth remembering as we strive to both expand and deepen the implementation of SEL in our nation's schools. And it speaks to the importance of this book in detailing what has worked for other districts. Personally, I have observed that the tipping point that often convinces us to adopt a new instructional practice is the results we see in our own students, thus the origin of the familiar advice to "change the behavior and beliefs will follow." Sometimes, you just have to jump in.

There are many potential places for a district or a school to start—all worthwhile. The starting point is usually in response to a locally felt need. Some points to consider before jumping: Will the structure of the proposed learning experience put students in a passive mode of listening, absorbing information, and following instructions or will it get them to think at a complex level and push them to be inquirers? Will the environment offer choices and teach students to take initiative and evaluate how the plans unfolded or will it teach them that they have to take direction from unquestioned others and conform? Will students be safe from humiliation or more subtle forms of being put down, excluded, or disregarded? On the positive side, will they be made to feel known and valued—and that they belong?

These messages have powerful effects on our students' attention, their self-image, their belief about their ability to learn, their sense of being valued, and the learning itself that they are absorbing about how to act as a person. What sophisticated practitioners such as Shelley have long understood is that these messages are sent through far more than direct lessons in purchased programs about social-emotional skills.

A comprehensive approach to SEL yields awareness of the many arenas in which social-emotional learning occurs and enhances our ability to be deliberate in how we structure them and interact within them. As the districts featured in this book have discovered, here are some facets to keep in mind when designing a districtwide approach to SEL.

- The selection of formal programs matters, but the professional learning of the educators implementing the programs matters more. At the heart of the process is a shift in how we approach children that brings curiosity, inquiry, empathetic listening, and trusting relationships to the forefront. This shift requires deep learning by the adults—and almost always entails unlearning some old habits.
- The routines for handling classroom business will change. An effective structure will deliberately build a community among the students where they know one another, feel safe in exposing their own vulnerabilities, and have social incentives for helping each other learn.
- Instructional practice will change. Inquiry-oriented experiences and the handling of disruptive behavior will be informed by teachers' capacity to facilitate robust student discussion. Classroom conversations will involve all students—not just some—in higher-level thinking and will teach skills in productive dialogue and conflict resolution.
- Words matter. The language of the classrooms embeds tacit messages about our view of students' ability. One example is the recommendation to use "yet" when describing students' incomplete journey to mastery. Adults' language must be congruent with

developing students' belief in themselves and motivating them to learn effective effort.
- SEL has intimate connections to other movements such as Deep Learning and Project-Based Learning, both of which help students make meaningful connections with the physical and political world, and Personalized Learning and Culturally Relevant Pedagogy, which use teachers' knowledge of individual students to adjust instruction and build supportive relationships. I point this out because each of these models is a complement to comprehensive SEL efforts and should not be seen as a competitor. So dig into these initiatives if they are already well underway in your district and search the case studies in this book for facets of SEL that can increase the complementary power of these movements.
- And finally, leadership matters. We need superintendents and other district leaders with longevity who will keep the focus on SEL and shifting the mindset. While superintendents can't do all the tasks, they need to be sure there is a person or group that will. One of the most important sustainability moves is forming communities of practice. Effective SEL leaders create an environment for the adults that mirrors the environment we want for students, knowing and valuing faculty members the way we want every student to feel known and valued in the classroom.

The district case studies in this book highlight many facets of the work in plain language and portray the different, usually messy, routes to success. The lessons are invaluable and deserve close reading. Shelley's experience brings enormous credibility to this analysis of the sustainable implementation of a vital movement of our era.

—Jon Saphier

Dr. Jon Saphier is the author of nine books, including *The Skillful Teacher* and *High Expectations Teaching*, and is the founder and president of Research for Better Teaching. Since 1979, he and his RBT colleagues have presented professional development programs—centered on the knowledge base of teaching—in hundreds of school districts in the United States and overseas.

Preface

As educators, most of us entered the field because of the joy we experience in our relationships with young people and because we hope to enrich their lives through learning experiences that hold meaning and value. Those were compelling passions for me. And probably like many of you, I also chose education because I felt driven to be involved in a career where I could make a positive and lasting difference in my small corner of the world. Although we usually don't give voice to this aspiration, I suspect that most educators share my hope for a ripple effect that, through those young lives, will help communities to become better places.

I began my career in education as a social studies teacher at Bangor High School in Maine. I had studied to become a guidance counselor; however, at that time state certification in guidance required three years of prior teaching experience. And so to move forward toward my counseling certificate, I accepted a position to teach the ninth-grade Current World Problems course with class sizes of thirty-five students or more.

Beyond the usual conveying of content, the task I was candidly assigned by my department head was to excite students about social studies. The goal was to motivate them to eagerly sign up for more social studies courses and thereby justify our current staffing. Since staffing in Bangor was allocated based on student enrollment within each department, the competitive environment among the departments was almost palpable. After all, our continued employment was at stake.

Being a novice teacher and feeling somewhat overwhelmed by the assignment, I walked into my classes and asked the students what issues in the world most concerned them. We created a list that varied from local to world issues. I asked them to prioritize the issues, and we launched into studying those that were at the top of their list.

Explaining that I wasn't an expert in the issues they listed, I shared with them that I would be learning alongside them. And so together we launched into powerful inquiry processes of collecting information, looking at multiple perspectives, listening to each other's viewpoints, and thinking critically not only about what we were discovering but also about potential solutions.

What I saw in my students at that time was a profound desire to understand themselves, their perspectives and beliefs, and their role in the world around them. They were concerned about injustice and caring for others and struggled to figure out where they stood ethically on personal, social, and political issues. What I also learned was that each one wanted to be known, valued, respected, and cared about by other students and by the adults in their lives.

Learning alongside them and working together to answer complicated questions and address complex personal, social, and ethical issues helped me build relationships of trust and respect. It made me realize that I loved connecting with students and watching them grow. I was essentially a counselor in another venue—an arena that gave me the opportunity to interact with far more students.

I also realized that teaching wasn't really about the subject matter, although the students' learning the subject matter was the end goal. Rather, teaching was about facilitating personal, social, and intellectual development. The environment and culture of the classroom were critical to facilitating that development as were the relationships between myself and my students and among students in the class. Learning is deeply personal and requires the trust and respect of others so that we can risk learning something new and make mistakes along the way. Relationships and the sense of community in the classroom open the doors to learning.

As time went on, I was fortunate to be able to add psychology courses to my class load, where again I observed my students' eagerness for self-discovery, connectedness, and ethical understanding. My students taught me much in those early years of teaching and have continued to do so throughout my career.

The indelible impression left by those years was that the social curriculum of the school was as essential as the academic curriculum in ensuring both student well-being and student academic success. That understanding led me to help found Educators for Social Responsibility (now Engaging Schools), which focused on social skill development. That same awareness accompanied me to the superintendency, where I felt I would have the opportunity to foster school environments that nurtured intellectual, social, and emotional growth.

In the four school districts I led across twenty-eight school years, I learned that exceptional social and emotional learning (SEL) programs exist to support student development. The districts I served in utilized different SEL programs, and I had the opportunity to see both the potential and the weaknesses in each. I observed that there was no one best program and that a layering or even combining of programs was essential. I also observed that continuity and consistency across the grades made a difference.

Yet, while these programs were well designed and well articulated, what mattered most in determining the degree of effectiveness was their on-the-ground implementation. The depth of knowledge and commitment among faculty and administrators could spell success or doom for any program's implementation. How to deepen that knowledge and commitment became the essential questions in each of my four districts, with many lessons learned along the way.

When I retired from the superintendency, Mort Sherman, the associate executive director at AASA, The School Superintendents Association, asked me to provide leadership for their SEL cohort of school districts and for a small SEL Impact Project grant from the Chan Zuckerberg Initiative (CZI). That grant served to support my consultation and coaching of a set of districts across eighteen months, culminating in a written report of the lessons learned from their implementation experiences.

What we realized in the process of working with these districts was that there was much more to say about implementation, its nuances, and its vulnerabilities. Simply issuing independent case study reports on the districts was an insufficient outcome. This recognition led to the writing of the book you are about to read, which is an effort to not only highlight the experiences of six districts, four of which participated in the CZI Impact Project grant, but also to cull insights from implementation research and the experiences of organizations in the field that are supporting districts as they implement SEL programming.

Therefore, this book isn't so much about what SEL is, what the research tells us about its impact, and which programs work and which don't—although the book does address those issues in brief. Rather, its main focus is the story of how districts go about implementing SEL programs and which strategies bear fruit and which are more challenging. Each of the featured districts is finding success, but that portrait of success is as varied as the districts themselves.

This book is not about theory but about practice and its evolution over time. For that reason, it's not a toolkit but rather stories that reveal lived experience in attempting to move this work forward. The districts highlighted here are not exemplars of perfection but rather works in progress, still learning and growing as they seek to serve students in the best way they can.

This book is a story about promoting systemic change in the mindset and capabilities of staff, in the structure of the district, and in the vision, mission, and policies that guide the district. Context and process are crucial since no two districts are alike and making judgments about implementation depends on the opportunities available at a point in time.

Many persons have earned my deepest gratitude for their support in helping me pull together the case studies and the lessons to be learned from the experience of these and other districts. First among them is Mort Sherman for his vision and his commitment to students' social and emotional growth as the foundation for all cognitive growth and academic achievement. It was Mort who pursued the original grant and provided me with the opportunity to share the insights from this work. I also thank CZI for their commitment to SEL, with a special nod to Tyler Sussman, CZI's program officer, for his support and encouragement during the grant-funded portion of this project.

I also want to acknowledge the openness, sincerity, and commitment of the leaders in each of the six districts with whom I communicated regularly as the work progressed and who opened their districts to site visits and meetings with administrators and teachers so that I could observe up close their ongoing work in SEL. The superintendents in these districts—Dan Bridges, Eric Gordon, Ryan Noss, Teresa Salazar, Theron Schutte, and Aaron Spence—provided valuable insights about both their successes and their struggles. The districts' SEL leads—Matt Cretsinger, Amy Lesan, Angelyn Nichols, Natalie Romero, Bill

Stencil, and Lisa Xagas—are courageous and thoughtful individuals who have guided the work of these districts in profoundly helpful ways and were gracious in sharing their insights and their challenges.

I thank the many school and district leaders and teachers whom I had the opportunity to interview and observe as I developed the case studies. And deep appreciation goes to Eliza Drummond, who served as my executive assistant when I was superintendent in Eugene, Oregon, and returned to work with me as an administrative assistant for the work on the CZI grant and the AASA SEL cohort. Her organizational skills helped the meetings and site visits to run smoothly and effectively.

A number of other people extended valuable advice and assistance along the way. These individuals include David Osher of the American Institutes for Research (AIR), Mark Greenberg at the University of Pennsylvania, and Adam Voight at Cleveland State University, all of whom provided me with research documents and evaluation data that gave greater depth to this work. Melissa Schlinger, Vice President of Innovations and Partnerships at the Collaborative for Academic, Social, and Emotional Learning (CASEL), was exceptional in giving me access to their evaluation documents and SEL toolkits and in talking with me about issues of implementation that CASEL has experienced in working with districts.

I would be remiss if I failed to acknowledge some of the founders in this field whom I've had the privilege of working with and learning from over the many years of my work in SEL—in particular, Eric Schaps, Linda Darling-Hammond, Chip Wood, Pamela Seigle, Larry Dieringer, Roger Weissberg, and Maurice Elias. These individuals deeply influenced the perspective I bring to this work and, as innovative leaders, have had a profound impact on the field as a whole.

A special note of appreciation is owed to two individuals in particular. Long-time colleague Joyce Barnes offered her wisdom and insights as an educator and administrator along with her exceptional talents as an editor throughout this entire book project. And my patient wife, Sarah Haavind, provided me with the social-emotional support and encouragement that prompted me to persevere through the many long hours devoted to the crafting of this book.

Finally, I thank you, the reader, for your interest in expanding your understanding of the nuts and bolts that are key to the effective implementation of SEL. Whatever your role in the field of education, I hope your knowledge and practice are enhanced by learning about others' experiences in this effort, and I hope the chapters that follow strengthen your commitment to advocate the inclusion of social-emotional learning throughout our nation's schools.

—Sheldon Berman

Chapter 1

Why Does SEL Matter?

This book focuses on how educators can effectively implement social-emotional learning (SEL) programs and approaches that create a more positive learning environment in classrooms and schools and help students become more successful in school, work, and life. By delving deeply into the implementation experience of six very diverse districts, the case studies in this book offer insights and lessons that will support others in initiating or enhancing their own efforts.

However, first things first. As Simon Sinek (2009) points out, successful implementation starts with a deep understanding of why an initiative is important coupled with a vision of what we seek to achieve. So, this book begins with an overview of *why* the implementation of SEL programs and approaches is so critical and, once the decision has been made to implement, *why* it is so important that we do it well.

THE SOCIAL AND EMOTIONAL LIFE OF THE CLASSROOM

While families are children's first and primary educators in social and emotional development, we need to recognize that classrooms and schools provide social and emotional instruction every minute of every day, whether those lessons are offered consciously or subconsciously. We set norms for behavior and participation. We establish a social structure that communicates who has authority and control as well as what is valued and what receives affirmation. We facilitate individual and group activities that promote particular social behaviors, such as competition or cooperation, engagement or passivity, resilience or defeatism.

As Phillip Jackson (1968) so accurately illuminated in his study of classrooms more than half a century ago, the social and emotional life in classrooms is often the "hidden curriculum" that teaches students what is acceptable and how to function within the classroom society. For Jackson's classrooms of the 1960s, those messages communicated that what was truly valued was passivity, obedience to authority, and compliance within an individualistic and highly competitive social structure.

If we are looking for different ends than those—for example, collaboration, engagement, voice, and agency—we have to ask ourselves, Does the social structure of the classroom and school teach and embody the social and emotional attributes that affirm these goals? Collaboration, engagement, voice, and agency all require social interaction, perspective-taking, and problem-solving skills to effectively work with others, self-reflection and self-management skills to understand and appreciate one's impact on others, and an understanding of one's emotions and those of others to foster mutual respect and resolve differences.

These skills are not present from birth but require conscious development as a result of direct teaching, modeling, and experiencing within the life of the classroom and school. In actuality, we already have a social-emotional learning curriculum operating in every classroom and every school. Our challenge now is to see it for what it is and to think carefully about what we want it to be so that we can foster in students the social and emotional competencies necessary for their ultimate success in life.

THE CLASSROOM AS COMMUNITY

We know that particular classroom practices and classroom cultures promote quality learning. When students experience a sense of community in which they feel known, included, valued, and cared about, they perform better academically. That sense of being a member of a caring classroom community enables students to take learning risks and make mistakes that are the essence of the learning process, knowing they have the support of their peers and teachers.

In one of the first major breakthrough research studies of comprehensive SEL programming in school districts, the Developmental

Studies Center (now the Center for the Collaborative Classroom) found that developing a sense of community in classrooms had a profound impact on the elementary-age students involved. The center reported that "the greater the sense of community among students in a program class, the more favorable their scores on measures of the tendency to help others, reactions to transgressions, reasoning about prosocial and moral issues, conflict resolution skill, democratic values, and reading comprehension" (Solomon et al., 1992, p. 56).

In addition, the center found that the impact continued well beyond the elementary years (Schaps et al., 2004). Therefore, a key reason *why* SEL is so critical is that it can provide a rich and productive learning environment that promotes cognitive and academic growth along with social and emotional capabilities.

THE INEXTRICABLE CONNECTION WITH COGNITIVE GROWTH

Yet, there is an even deeper level of interdependence between the cognitive and the social and emotional elements of learning—a level that goes beyond the culture and structure of the classroom and school. Every step in the learning process has both social and emotional components. In fact, you cannot divorce cognitive growth from its social and emotional partners. Cognitive growth and development occur both within and as a result of a social context. We certainly learn by observing others, but often we learn much more by engaging with them. In addition, every learning experience involves emotion, whether that emotion is the frustration at failure, the pride in success, or the joy of an "aha" moment when a new insight emerges.

The National Commission on Social, Emotional, and Academic Development convened a Council of Distinguished Scientists comprising twenty-eight nationally known researchers, scientists, and scholars from such diverse fields as medicine, neuroscience, psychology, sociology, and education. The Council was charged with coming to a consensus about what the research in social and emotional learning tells us. In their report, these experts point to the intimate connection between the cognitive and the social and emotional aspects of learning.

One of their prime conclusions is that "the major domains of human development—social, emotional, cognitive, linguistic, academic—are deeply intertwined in the brain and in behavior. All are central to learning. Strengths or weaknesses in one area foster or impede development in others; each carries aspects of the other" (Jones and Kahn, 2017, p. 4).

Understanding the deep connections among the social, emotional, and cognitive elements of learning requires us to design instruction consciously with each of these elements in mind in order to create the most constructive learning experiences for our students. It also means that, through our daily instruction, we need to help students learn the self-awareness, self-management, social-awareness, and social problem-solving skills that enable them to take learning risks, cope with frustration, persist through challenges, and engage in collaborative learning so that we maximize the potential for productive learning.

As Linda Darling-Hammond and the Learning Policy Institute have pointed out, the research affirms the connections among cognitive, social, and emotional learning. The research also highlights the vital importance of helping students develop the social and emotional skills that best facilitate their own learning (Darling-Hammond et al., 2020; Learning Policy Institute & Turnaround for Children, 2021).

IMPACTS AFFIRMED BY RESEARCH

The impact of effective implementation of social-emotional learning programs on students is profound and, fortunately, well documented by hundreds of research studies. In fact, the very history of the field of social-emotional learning is rooted in science. Two individuals who helped launch the field, Roger Weissberg and Eric Schaps, were both prevention researchers whose studies pointed to the indispensable value of SEL in child development and learning. They also knew that unless hard science supported the necessity of focusing on social and emotional development as essential for academic learning as well as life skill development, this area would be seen as "soft skills" rather than as a crucial and strategic priority for educators.

Roger Weissberg, the founder of the Collaborative for Academic, Social, and Emotional Learning (CASEL) and a prevention researcher himself, drew together other key researchers in the prevention field. Along with Mark Greenberg, Maurice Elias, Joseph Durlak, Joseph

Zins, and others, Weissberg launched CASEL on a foundation of prevention science (Elias et al., 1997).

Eric Schaps, the president and founder of the Developmental Studies Center, created and studied one of the first comprehensive, school-wide, social-emotional learning programs—the Child Development Project. Through this research, he and his research colleagues were able to document the powerful impact social-emotional learning can have on students' social and academic development (Schaps et al., 2004; Solomon et al., 2000; Watson et al., 1997).

Since those early years, the research foundation underlying social-emotional learning has been further strengthened by thirteen meta-analyses: seven examining programs at all grade levels, four focused on preschool, and two focused on secondary school. Collectively, they cover research conducted in the United States, Europe, Australia, and Asia (Greenberg, 2023; Cipriano et al., under review). This work affirms the important influence evidence-based programming in social-emotional learning can have on youth development.

In their 2011 breakthrough meta-analysis of 213 studies conducted through 2008, Joseph Durlak and his colleagues found that "SEL programs yielded significant positive effects on targeted social-emotional competencies and attitudes about self, others, and school. The programs also enhanced students' behavioral adjustment in the form of increased prosocial behaviors and reduced conduct and internalized problems, and improved academic performance on achievement tests and grades" (Durlak et al., 2011, p. 417). The researchers also found that SEL programs were most effective when they offered a coordinated and sequenced set of activities, used active forms of learning, focused on developing personal and social skills, and explicitly targeted specific SEL skills. They labeled these the "SAFE" criteria—an acronym for sequenced, active, focused, and explicit (Durlak et al., 2011, p. 417).

In terms of the academic impact, these researchers noted that "the 11-percentile gain in academic performance achieved in these programs is noteworthy.... Educators who are pressured ... to improve the academic performance of their students might well welcome programs that could boost achievement by 11 percentile points" (Durlak et al., 2011, p. 417). Alexandru Boncu and his colleagues in Romania picked up where Durlak's meta-analysis left off, focusing on studies conducted between 2008 and 2015. Their findings essentially affirm the earlier results but note stronger effects in early childhood and elementary grades (Boncu et al., 2017).

Both the social and the academic impacts revealed in Durlak's meta-analysis are further confirmed by additional meta-analyses. Michael Wigelsworth and his colleagues (2016) synthesized data from eighty-nine studies and found statistically significant benefits for participating students. Meta-analyses by Marcin Sklad and his colleagues (2012) and by Rebecca Taylor and her colleagues (2017) focused on the longer-term effects of social-emotional learning programs, with reviews of seventy-five studies and eighty-two studies, respectively. They found continued impact after the programs ended, particularly in the area of academic achievement (Sklad et al., 2012; Taylor et al., 2017; Wigelsworth et al., 2016).

Roisin Corcoran and her colleagues reviewed forty studies focusing on academic outcomes and found significant effects on both mathematics and reading performance (Corcoran et al., 2018). Jochem Goldberg and his colleagues examined forty-five studies of whole-school social-emotional programs, finding similar results to prior meta-analyses (Goldberg et al., 2019). The four meta-analyses that focused on preschool-age programs (Blewitt et al., 2018; Luo et al., 2022; Murano et al., 2020; Yang et al., 2019) consistently found that SEL programs improved social and emotional competencies and decreased challenging behaviors and conduct problems.

The two meta-analyses of secondary school programs also showed significant impacts. Marion van de Sande and her colleagues found positive outcomes on social and emotional competencies as well as reduction in depression, anxiety, substance use, and aggression (van de Sande et al., 2019). Esther Mertens and her colleagues found significant effects on students' intrapersonal and interpersonal skills, with stronger effects seen in programs that were longer in duration and included opportunities to practice skills, problem-solve, and build insight (Mertens et al., 2022).

Mark Greenberg, in his review of all twelve of the meta-analyses, concludes that "it is clear from the twelve meta-analyses that examined hundreds of studies that there is a consistent, reliable effect of evidence-based SEL programs on students' social, emotional, behavioral, and academic outcomes across all grade levels from pre-K through grade 12 and across gender, ethnicity/race, income, and other demographic variables" (Greenberg, 2023, p. 11).

Christina Cipriano and her colleagues (2023) sought to update and extend the Durlak et al. (2011) study, reviewing 424 SEL-related studies from fifty-three countries completed between 2008 and 2020. Given the substantial changes in educational policy and practice around SEL and its growing prevalence worldwide, they felt that more recent evidence and a more detailed analysis would provide further insight not only into the impact of SEL but also into the factors that support stronger outcomes.

Cipriano et al. (2023) report that SEL interventions produced statistically significant improvements in academic achievement, social-emotional skills, and prosocial and civic behavior, while reducing problems with internalization and externalization. One of the most significant findings in their meta-analysis is that SEL programs had a positive impact on school climate and students' sense of safety, affirming earlier research in this area (Berg et al., 2017; Wang et al., 2020). In addition, Cipriano et al. (2023) confirmed Durlak's (2011) finding that programs that met the SAFE criteria had higher quality implementation and stronger impact on students.

SEL also benefits the teachers who are implementing programs in their classrooms. Schaps found that participating in the Child Development Project had a positive impact on teachers' classroom practices (Schaps et al., 2004). Other researchers have uncovered similar results. For example, SEL programs have had a positive influence not only on classroom climate, but also on teacher effectiveness (Brackett et al., 2012; Greenberg et al., 2003; Hagelskamp et al., 2013; Rivers et al., 2013).

Greenberg et al. (2016), in a meta-analysis on teacher stress and health, found that teachers trained and supported in implementing SEL programs had improved management of student behaviors, higher quality classroom interactions with students, greater perceived job control, lower job-related anxiety, and higher levels of personal accomplishment. In essence, SEL training for teachers and the implementation of SEL programs in their classrooms created environments that supported adults as well as students by improving teacher efficacy and satisfaction, school climate, and teacher morale.

STEPPINGSTONE TO EQUITY

We continue to live and work in a socially stratified society with highly divergent outcomes for students of color and students impacted by poverty. We still labor to close achievement and opportunity gaps and create more equitable and inclusive environments in which all students succeed. SEL can be an essential lever in creating those more equitable learning environments. When SEL is approached as building on students' strengths and assets and when it focuses on fixing the learning environment rather than fixing the student, we are able to create positive learning environments that welcome and strengthen diversity.

The goal of social-emotional learning in America's diverse classrooms is to ensure that every student, regardless of cultural, racial, or socioeconomic differences, is infused with a sense of personal belonging, safety, and respect that promotes the freedom to learn. While it is not realistic to expect that SEL can eliminate all the inequities found in educational settings—especially those flowing from institutional bias or funding disparities—it can flip the focus from the qualities that students may lack to the assets that every student brings as a result of their lived experiences.

SEL brings a consciousness of and openness to the rich human diversity found in thousands of American classrooms. Many of the cultures represented therein are strikingly different from each other and may be more communitarian than the United States' traditional individualism. When that diversity is not acknowledged, the classroom environment can become one that accepts, projects, and inculcates the dominant social values, norms, and mores, thereby making some children feel isolated, unsupported, and unseen. In contrast, by recognizing and welcoming the multiplicity of cultures represented in the classroom, teachers can leverage diversity to enhance student engagement, broaden perspectives, and enrich relationships.

A classroom that is steeped in social-emotional learning supports positive relationships among all students, particularly those who have traditionally been marginalized. Such a learning environment models the behaviors that students can apply in other settings to bring compassion, equity, and a sense of responsibility to the world around them (Berman, 2021).

CIVIC ENGAGEMENT AND RESPONSIBILITY

So, in essence, the *why* of SEL implementation in schools is to enable all students to develop the skills to maximize their ability to learn and to enable educators to create highly productive and equitable learning environments. There are numerous other *why* reasons that emerge from the research literature, such as enhancing students' mental health and emotional well-being, their preparation for success in career and work environments, and their ability to maintain positive relationships. However, there is another reason that has particular importance to our society as a whole.

Our work in helping young people develop social and emotional skills and our work to create caring classroom communities enables students to become more engaged and effective community members and citizens. In fact, SEL develops in students a social consciousness and sense of social responsibility so that they are better able to develop a moral compass and make ethically grounded decisions that sustain and enrich our democratic society.

Ultimately, public education in a democratic society has one primary goal: to enable young people to develop into thoughtful, compassionate, well-informed, and engaged citizens who constructively participate in the life of their communities, states, and country. This mission is embodied in the vision and mission statements of nearly every school district in the United States, and frankly should be the objective of all education—whether public, charter, or private—in a democratic society.

Responsible civic participation requires more than acquiring academic knowledge. It requires empathy and the capacity to take the perspective of others. It requires the ability to work with others, resolve conflicts, and find common ground. It requires effective problem-solving and decision-making skills. It requires understanding what it means to be a member of a community that places a value on the common good of all in the community.

All of these traits represent the social and emotional skills that are embodied in social-emotional learning. These are the skills that enable communities to grow and prosper and ensure that democratic governance thrives. Although these skills may not always appear to be well represented in our current political culture of polarization and division, they are the skills that bring us together to resolve differences and work toward common goals.

Many school districts' vision and mission statements aspire to this ultimate goal of positive civic engagement and responsible citizenship. For example, in Andover, Massachusetts, the district's theory of action and mission statement closed with this: "We will provide every student with opportunities and support to . . . demonstrate cultural awareness, an appreciation of self, empathy toward others, a sense of responsibility, and commitment to civic engagement." The theme of constructive civic participation is echoed in the vast majority of district and school mission statements, in their portraits of a graduate, and in their strategic planning documents.

As educators and as leaders, our work in fostering social and emotional development in young people is inextricably linked to the very mission of public education, the heart of our communities, and the vitality of our democratic culture. As the Council of Distinguished Educators stated in its report to the National Commission on Social, Emotional, and Academic Development:

> As educators, we envision a world in which students graduate from high school not only prepared for college and career, but accepting their responsibility to take an active role in their communities and contribute to civic life. We envision a world of principled, compassionate civility, where students learn through guided practice in real-life situations how to engage in open dialogue and to treat one another with dignity and mutual respect. We envision a world in which school is where children learn how to be the best possible versions of themselves and to pursue the positive difference they can make in the world. We see the integration of social, emotional, and academic development as the pathway to learning that achieves these ends. (Berman et al., 2018, p. 4)

Chapter 2

What Is SEL?

The "why" of social and emotional learning is inspiring, but now let's consider more precisely "what" SEL is, especially in the classroom setting. *What* are the social and emotional competencies and skills that define our learning targets, and *what* are the strategies and approaches that cultivate those competencies and skills? *What* does effective SEL look like—not in a textbook but on the ground?

SOCIAL AND EMOTIONAL COMPETENCIES AND SKILLS

CASEL (Collaborative for Academic, Social, and Emotional Learning) defines social-emotional learning as

> the process through which all young people and adults acquire and apply the knowledge, skills, and attitudes to develop healthy identities, manage emotions and achieve personal and collective goals, feel and show empathy for others, establish and maintain supportive relationships, and make responsible and caring decisions. (CASEL, n.d.)

Many school districts and SEL programs utilize the CASEL framework (see figure 2.1) and the five competencies of self-awareness, self-management, social awareness, relationship skills, and responsible decision-making as curriculum standards to guide instruction.

The five core competencies are general concepts that are useful for categorizing a range of intra- and interpersonal knowledge, skills, and abilities (Weissberg et al., 2015).

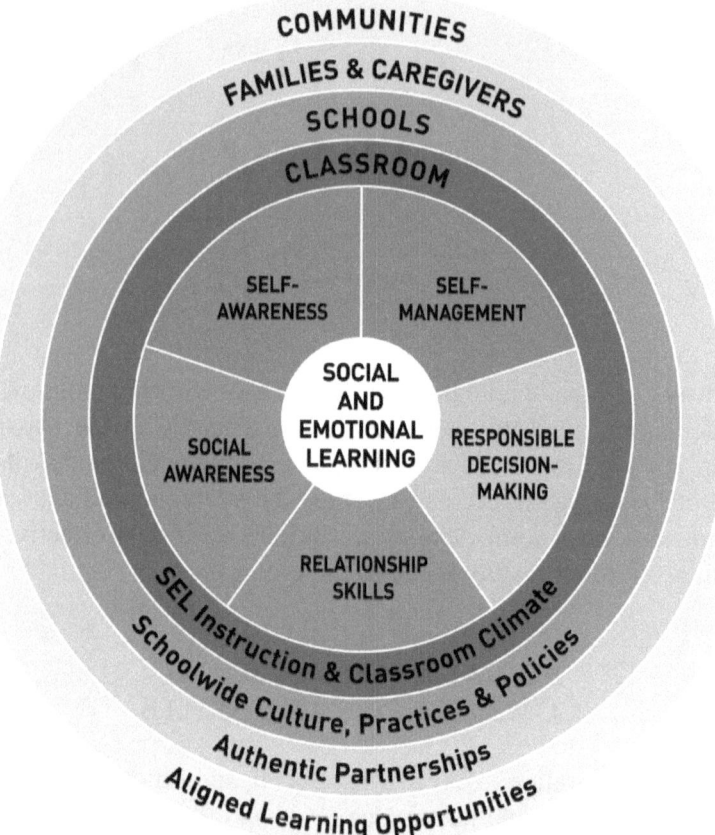

Figure 2.1. Social and Emotional Learning Framework (the CASEL Wheel, 2020). Reprinted with permission from the Collaborative for Academic, Social, and Emotional Learning (CASEL).

Self-awareness, for example, involves the ability to identify one's thoughts, emotions, strengths, limitations, and values, and to become aware of one's identity and how identity influences one's choices and behavior. It includes developing a positive mindset and a sense of self-efficacy. There is a developmental process for each of the competencies. For self-awareness, that development includes becoming aware of one's biases, how one's personal history is interwoven with one's cultural and social context, and how thoughts, feelings, and actions are interconnected.

The domain of self-management encompasses the ability to effectively regulate and manage one's emotions, thoughts, and behaviors in different situations. It includes the ability to control impulses, manage stress, cope with disappointment, and delay gratification in pursuit of goals and aspirations. As individuals develop self-management, they also develop the ability to set, monitor, evaluate, and adjust personal goals and to advocate on their own behalf.

Social awareness entails the ability to identify and understand the thoughts, emotions, and actions of others, as well as to take the perspective of others, empathize, and express gratitude and compassion. Developmentally, it involves understanding and reflecting on social norms, respecting differences, appreciating cultural diversity, and becoming aware of one's relationship to and responsibility in community, national, and global issues and events.

Relationship skills involve the ability to establish and maintain healthy and responsive relationships with individuals and groups. This domain includes skills in communication, active listening, collaboration, cooperative problem-solving, and constructive resolution of conflict. As individuals develop, they increase their ability to effectively manage complex relationship issues, resist inappropriate social pressure, negotiate differences, and provide constructive leadership in social situations.

Finally, the domain of responsible decision-making encompasses making caring and constructive choices in both personal and social situations. It consists of the ability to think critically about one's choices, to reflect on one's attitudes and actions, and to gather, analyze, and evaluate information in order to make positive choices, as well as to appreciate the impact of those choices on others. Responsible decision-making grows over time to include considerations of social norms, ethical standards, safety concerns, and concern for the common good, and it expands to consider one's obligation to the well-being of the larger society.

The five domains are not independent of each other but rather are interdependent and synergistic. However, their categorization into these domains has enabled states and school districts to set standards and learning targets on a more defined and focused basis.

By adding attention to issues of equity, the scope of each of these five domains reaches beyond simply personal and interpersonal skills to encompass an individual's responsibility to and effectiveness in the larger social and political arena (Jagers et al., 2019). In CASEL's framework, skill development is facilitated by each of the environments in which students spend time—in the classroom and school, with their families and caregivers, and in the community at large.

Stephanie Jones and her colleagues at the Harvard Graduate School of Education's EASEL (Ecological Approaches to Social Emotional Learning) Laboratory took an approach that is somewhat different than CASEL's set of social-emotional competencies. Instead, the EASEL Lab team outlined six categories of skills and beliefs (Jones et al., 2021). Based on this framework, the team reviewed thirty-three of the most frequently used elementary SEL programs to identify each program's areas of emphasis. The categories themselves provide a sense of the breadth of skills and competencies involved in social and emotional development.

The first three of the EASEL Lab's six categories directly relate to specific competencies and include the following:

1. *Cognitive skills* such as attention control, inhibitory control, working memory and planning skills, cognitive flexibility, and critical thinking. These can be thought of as the skills needed to focus and manage one's emotions and behaviors in order to achieve a goal.
2. *Emotional skills* such as emotional knowledge and expression, emotional and behavioral regulation, and empathy and perspective-taking. These skills help people recognize, express, and control their emotions and understand the emotions of others.
3. *Social skills* such as understanding social cues, conflict resolution, social problem-solving, and prosocial and cooperative behavior. These skills enable people to effectively develop and navigate relationships and work cooperatively with others.

In addition, the EASEL Lab found that there is a "belief ecology" of values, perspectives, and identity that strongly influences how people view themselves and the world around them. "Belief ecologies not only influence our ability to develop and deploy the skills included in the cognitive, social, and emotional domains, but also how we ultimately decide to use those skills, such as whether we use strong perspective-taking skills to empathize with the feelings of others vs. to take advantage of them" (Jones et al., 2021, p. 17).

This belief ecology encompasses the EASEL Lab's other three categories:

4. *Values* such as ethical, performance, civic, and intellectual values. These values are interrelated and guide an individual's approach to prosocial action, community participation, intellectual honesty, concern for the welfare of others, and the pursuit of truth.
5. *Perspectives* such as one's attitudes, mindsets, and outlooks on gratitude, openness, optimism, and enthusiasm or zest. These perspectives define how a child views and approaches the world, how they see themselves and others, and how they respond to events and interactions.
6. *Identity* in terms of how children understand and perceive their abilities through self-knowledge, purpose, self-efficacy/growth mindset, and self-esteem. Children's positive sense of identity enables them to overcome obstacles and cope with challenges in order to learn and grow.

These values, perspectives, and identity form children's social consciousness, that is, their sense of relatedness to and affiliation with the social world around them, and they influence the development of a sense of social responsibility (Berman, 1997). These characteristics are much more subtle features of SEL programs than are the cognitive, social, and emotional skills, yet they are no less important.

Many of the SEL programs used by the districts profiled in this book have been reviewed by the EASEL Lab team. Others have been reviewed by CASEL to determine whether they are evidence-based programs that demonstrate a research-based positive impact on student development. Where the programs have been reviewed, the following chapters will discuss the evidence documented by CASEL and the emphases identified by the EASEL Lab team, as well as the implications for the impact that each program's emphases may have had on the district's SEL programming.

The CASEL framework has become the dominant one in the formation of state and district social-emotional learning standards. However, there are other constructs beyond those of CASEL or Jones that districts and programs have selected to use as their standards. As of the writing of this book, twenty-seven states have adopted SEL standards to guide instruction and SEL implementation.

No matter which framework or set of standards a district selects, it serves as an important guide as the district defines the learning targets of instruction, the design of instructional activities, the approach to assessment and progress monitoring, and the content for professional development of faculty and staff. Therefore, clarity around both the SEL framework and the areas of emphasis in commercial and district-designed programs is critical to ensuring a comprehensive approach that addresses the broad range of social and emotional competencies and skills.

STRATEGIES TO DELIVER RESULTS

The National Commission on Social, Emotional, and Academic Development formed a Council of Distinguished Educators to answer questions about which SEL strategies best deliver the desired results. This council involved more than thirty educators from diverse roles and regions in developing a consensus on the essential strategies that promote positive social and emotional development. After extensive investigation, the educators council identified four strategies that meet the criterion—direct instruction, building a sense of community in classrooms, integration into academic instruction, and service learning.

Although schools and districts may place an emphasis on one or another of these strategies, none of them is exclusive of the others. In fact, they all work best when applied in tandem to create a comprehensive approach to social and emotional development in young people.

DIRECT INSTRUCTION

The value of direct instruction is that it specifically focuses instruction on sets of social and emotional skills and competencies, identifying key language, providing skill development experiences, and enabling students to apply their learning to real-life situations in the classroom, on the playground, and in other school-related areas and events.

Numerous curricular programs offer direct skill instruction, each taking a somewhat different approach. Some focus more on social decision-making and conflict-resolution skills, while others concentrate on emotional awareness and management, and still others emphasize executive functioning and self-regulation.

In addition, the direct skills instruction programs vary on how they are implemented. Some, particularly at the elementary level, establish a cadence of weekly lessons, twenty to forty minutes in length. Typically, each lesson is scripted for teachers and may engage students in interpreting social situations, role playing those situations, and discussing alternative ways to best address each situation productively.

The lessons are generally interactive and involve discussion and problem solving. The theme of the lesson is then revisited throughout the week through literature, activities that highlight the theme, or natural situations that emerge in the life of the classroom. The programs almost always include a scope and sequence based on standards that deepen and extend social and emotional skill development across grade levels. In essence, direct instruction can help students understand why a skill is important and how to use it effectively through engagement and practice.

BUILDING COMMUNITY IN CLASSROOMS AND SCHOOLS

Direct instruction can lay a strong foundation for the development of social and emotional competencies. However, to effectively nurture these skills, the classroom itself must embody and exemplify the positive social and emotional skills we strive to teach. In effect, the classroom setting should be perceived as a key player in the quest for high-level SEL because it has the capacity to provide an interactive and relationship-centered learning environment for the ongoing development of academic, emotional, and social skills.

The day-to-day environment of the classroom communicates to students the social norms and behaviors that are valued and respected. The way the classroom is structured, the way teachers interact with students, and the way students are taught to interact with each other can either foster or undermine the development of social and emotional skills. Students can best learn social and emotional skills by living them in the classroom and seeing the consequences of specific behaviors.

One of the key vehicles for effectively teaching positive social and emotional skills is through the building of a sense of community in classrooms. When students experience a sense of community, they become more aware of their interconnections and relationships with others. They observe how their actions, and failures to act, impact others. The situations they face within a community are real situations that necessitate negotiation, conflict resolution, and collaboration. They also require empathy, perspective-taking, and respect.

Essentially, within a classroom that embodies the elements of community, students experience being valued and influential contributors to a group that is dedicated to the learning and well-being of all of its members. In such a setting, social and emotional competencies are modeled by both adults and students daily.

To create and continually foster that sense of community, teachers must ensure that students feel a sense of connection to others in the classroom. They need to feel known, valued, cared about, and respected. The classroom needs to be inclusive of differences—whether of culture, race, ethnicity, sexual orientation, or ability—by honoring and appreciating the varied contributions individuals can bring to the classroom based on their cultural and racial backgrounds and their lived experiences.

Being a member of a community also requires that students have voice, influence, and agency within the classroom. In some cases that experience is embodied in students' contributions to setting the norms or rules for the classroom and then having discussions when there is a transgression of those norms. In other cases, it involves an ongoing dialogue about how well the classroom is facilitating learning for students. Choice is critical to developing agency, so creating an inclusive community also means teachers must offer choices of multiple ways students can learn material and express what they know.

The essential program strategies for creating that sense of community are through regular gatherings of the entire class for morning meetings, closing meetings, and class meetings. Morning meetings, particularly at the elementary level, are daily gatherings that create a positive climate in the classroom through activities that engage students in getting to know each other—activities such as greetings, short games, and individual sharing. Often this is a time when the teacher can talk about the agenda for the day so that students have an idea of what to expect. Just being aware of what the day's activities will entail gives students a sense of self-control and agency.

Closing meetings again bring the class together as a community, this time so students can share an insight or experience from the day, prior to dismissal. Finally, class meetings are opportunities for the class to gather for the purpose of planning new initiatives and opportunities, solving class problems, and discussing strategies to help the class become more inclusive and successful. At the beginning of the year, these meetings are often used to enable students to help set the norms for the classroom.

Community is also built through the very design of instruction. Intentional design can include such strategies as collaborative activities in which students learn to support each other's learning, activity centers that offer students choices in how they will learn material, and teachers breaking from the typical teacher-centered discussion protocol and instead encouraging students to build on each other's thinking. These strategies will be more fully discussed in the next section.

Finally, the systems for behavior management and discipline are different in a classroom that is functioning as a community. Punishment and exclusion are not the primary modes of discipline. Instead, when there is an infraction, violation of norms, inappropriate action, or harm done to another, the incident provides an opportunity for learning and self-correcting through apologies and restitution. The goal is not only to improve one's social skills so that the mistake won't be repeated, but to act in a way that enables the student to reenter the community with dignity.

As pointed out in the first chapter, the very process of creating a caring and inclusive classroom community can have a powerful impact on the development of social and emotional competencies. This process represents the core of such programs as Responsive Classroom and Caring School Community. The National Commission on Social, Emotional, and Academic Development reported that

> [r]esearch provides clear direction for instruction that best supports student engagement and intellectual risk taking, and for the environments that foster strong learning communities. The way teachers and administrators interact with students, facilitate relationships among students, and model positive relationship-building plays a critical role in students' sense of belonging, emotional safety, ability to collaborate with peers, and identities as learners. (Berman et al., 2018, p. 6)

INTEGRATION INTO ACADEMIC INSTRUCTION

When it comes to fostering social and emotional competencies, how we teach can be as instrumental as what we teach. A third strategy for facilitating the development of social and emotional competencies is to integrate them into everyday academic instruction. Teachers can incorporate classroom interaction that supports the development of these skills. Using cooperative learning activities, Socratic seminars, project-based learning, and other interactive activities provides students with the opportunity to share ideas, discuss divergent perspectives, resolve differences, and build on each other's thinking.

Each of these activities requires social skills that can be taught as part of the lesson itself and refined as students reflect on their interactions with others. However, this approach demands conscious effort on the part of the teacher to target specific social competencies within the lesson, explicitly elaborate on the social skill focus of the lesson with students, make instruction of that skill explicit within the unfolding of the lesson, and engage students in assessing how well they met expectations to demonstrate the skill.

Embedding social and emotional development within instruction in this way takes time and intention, but also enables students to see and experience the utility of these skills as they work together to achieve their academic goals. In addition, as students develop these competencies, their improved proficiency enhances the climate of the classroom and supports a more engaging and productive learning environment.

In addition to integrating social skill strategies into the instructional design of lessons, the academic content in each curricular area offers opportunities to highlight social and emotional competencies. For example, fictional literature offers teachers an opportunity to highlight the social situations within a novel or short story and how characters managed each situation and their emotions. Students can then discuss alternative strategies for managing such situations, as well as where comparable situations might emerge in their own lives.

Similarly, history and social studies offer rich opportunities to help students reflect on conflict escalation and conflict resolution as well as the ways individuals, whether historical or contemporary, exhibit or fail to exhibit appropriate social and emotional skills and the consequences of these actions.

Science presents a highly respected and effective way for thinking through problems by testing hypotheses through investigation, observation, and experimental evidence prior to making judgments. It also presents science-based social and political dilemmas, such as climate change or energy conservation, that require social and emotional competencies as well as academic knowledge and critical thinking to solve. Even mathematics presents opportunities to highlight multiple ways to think through and solve a problem.

The arts offer many opportunities not only for expressing emotion and presenting perspectives on social situations but also for analyzing the social and emotional perspectives raised by artists in their works. Meanwhile, social and emotional competencies are at the core of health and physical education curricula, where topics related to social pressure, risk, and well-being are discussed and where cooperation and sportsmanship are taught.

Some publishers have now begun to integrate the teaching of social and emotional skills within their programs' academic lessons and units. One example is the Collaborative Literacy program provided by the Center for the Collaborative Classroom. As elementary teachers deliver lessons in reading and writing, the activities are designed to be collaborative, the social competencies to be taught are highlighted, and the lesson plans guide the teacher on how to best teach those social competencies while enhancing students' reading proficiency. The program's literary selections provide examples of social dilemmas that characters have to grapple with, along with models of how social skills can be applied effectively.

Other publishers may not be as explicit, but many are beginning to address social and emotional competencies as part of their approach to academic instruction. However, even if a curricular program provides the opportunity to address social and emotional development, to meaningfully integrate the discussion and development of social and emotional competencies through the curriculum requires that teachers take the time to ensure that lesson plans and curriculum guides explicitly highlight these strategies as an essential part of the lesson.

COMMUNITY SERVICE AND SERVICE LEARNING

To develop social and emotional competencies in a way that ingrains them into daily behavior, students need opportunities to exhibit their learning beyond the classroom environment. Two highly effective ways for students to express their empathy, perspective-taking, and caring are through active engagement in both community service and service learning (Celio et al., 2011; Yorio & Ye, 2012).

Both types of classroom- and school-generated activity enable students to demonstrate their social and emotional skills, recognize the value of the common good, and help others in need. And both afford a public forum where students can apply their developing social and emotional skills, be affirmed for these efforts, and become more confident of their ability to make meaningful contributions to society at large.

Community service involves acts of service such as food and clothing drives or fund-raising for victims of natural or human disasters. These positive actions on the part of individuals may be school sponsored but are generally independent of the curriculum. In service learning, on the other hand, students study an issue that is directly tied to the curriculum and then engage in service as an authentic avenue for demonstrating both their understanding of the issue and of ways that individuals can make a difference on that issue. Teachers can integrate service-learning activities into instruction in any curricular area, and schools can offer opportunities for students to participate in community service activities that support community needs.

Not only do assisting others in need and addressing community issues give students the opportunity to express empathy, compassion, and responsibility, but these efforts strengthen students' self-esteem, self-confidence, and sense of efficacy. As with other learning activities, the development of specific social and emotional competencies can be built into service-learning lessons.

For example, in a service-learning project in social studies, students may interview war veterans and practice their listening and perspective-taking skills. A reading buddies program that pairs fifth graders with second graders, fourth graders with first graders, and third graders with kindergarten students not only helps younger children learn to enjoy reading and older students to enhance their own reading skills, it extends an opportunity for children of all ages to model positive social skills. It also gives upper-grade students the opportunity to refine their prosocial behavior.

Community service and service learning constitute important strategies for teaching and affirming social and emotional competencies. "These [service-learning] opportunities allow students to use and generalize their SEL skills in 'real world' settings that are both personally relevant and can open opportunities for the future" (Mahoney et al., 2020, p. 10).

MUTUALLY SUPPORTIVE STRATEGIES

Direct instruction, building a sense of community in classrooms, integrating social and emotional competencies into academic instruction, and service learning can be pursued independently. However, they achieve the best and most lasting results when undertaken in conjunction with each other. None is exclusive of the others.

As the reader will see in the case studies described in this book, districts start their SEL implementation journey in different places with different approaches. Over time, as districts deepen their SEL programming, they reach into the implementation of the other strategies as a way to provide a more comprehensive, cohesive, and coherent approach to the development of social and emotional competencies.

What becomes clear is that the social curriculum of the school is a critical, mutually supportive partner of the academic curriculum. It creates and sustains a positive learning environment while promoting student development. To do it well requires the same thoughtfulness, planning, and professional development that we devote to the academic curriculum.

Chapter 3

How Should We Implement SEL?

WHAT THE RESEARCH TELLS US

The *how* of program implementation is both a science and an art. Over the past several decades, the field of implementation science has grown dramatically, providing insight into the critical factors and conditions that facilitate effective and sustainable implementation of evidence-based programs (Lyon, 2017; Moir, 2018).

IMPLEMENTATION MODELS FOR EDUCATIONAL SETTINGS

Seeking to overcome the challenges of bridging research to practice and science to service, the field has sought to identify models and methods that enable practitioners to implement and scale interventions and innovations with fidelity to their intended outcome. Models for effective implementation emerging from this field have proliferated as theorists and researchers have struggled to come to terms with the complexity inherent in social and institutional change. In fact, researchers have identified more than sixty of these models in the implementation literature (Tabak et al., 2012).

   A number of these models have been applied to educational settings, each taking a different approach to helping practitioners develop implementation plans.

- *The Exploration, Preparation, Implementation, Sustainability (EPIS) Framework* highlights four key phases of implementation and the bridging factors between evidence-based practice and the context of the setting.
- *The National Implementation Research Network's (NIRN) Active Implementation Framework (AIF)* explicates five core components of implementation—a usable innovation, implementation drivers or rationales and motivations for implementation, overlapping implementation stages, improvement cycles, and implementation teams.
- *The Interactive Systems Framework (ISF)* focuses on the gap between the development of an intervention and its widespread adoption by examining the systems for translating scientific knowledge into understandable and actionable information, building capacity for implementation within an organization, and providing the infrastructure for effective delivery of the practice.
- *The Consolidated Framework for Implementation Research (CFIR)* provides a set of constructs to consider when planning implementations, such as the attributes of the intervention that can influence its implementation; the navigation necessary to accommodate both outer and inner organizational settings; indicators of readiness and commitment to adopt the intervention; the nature of the interplay between individuals, their teams, their departments, and the overall organization; and the process of planning, engaging, executing, and reflecting on and evaluating the intervention.

As is evidenced by the diversity and complexity of each of these models, effective implementation is a multi-faceted challenge requiring forethought and planning. However, three common insights emerge. The models agree that implementation takes place in stages or phases over time; it needs to occur at multiple levels at the same time within complex systems; and there is a significant contextual relationship between the practice to be implemented and the organizational conditions that mediate its adoption and adaptation (Lyon, 2017).

IMPLEMENTATION FRAMEWORKS FOR SEL

Both CASEL and AASA have developed their own implementation frameworks to support districtwide implementation of SEL programs. CASEL's District Resource Center provides a framework built around three core phases: organize, execute, and improve.

The key to the first phase—effective organizing—is to launch SEL with a clear vision, a robust plan, and adequate resources. Therefore, organizing begins with establishing a shared vision and plan based on an assessment of need and the resources available to carry out the plan. Planning includes providing a systemic approach to implementation that aligns both financial and human resources, as well as outlining the system for data collection and progress monitoring to build a continuous improvement cycle. Communication is key in this phase so that stakeholders within and outside the organization appreciate the priority being given to SEL.

The execution phase begins with a focus on developing and/or strengthening competencies and capacities of the adults in the system—teachers, support staff, and school-based and district-level administrators. Developing central office expertise is essential for effective leadership of program implementation. It leads to the design and implementation of multiple systems for structured in-service and embedded professional learning for school staff. The goal is not only to grow staff capabilities to deliver SEL programming, but to strengthen adults' own social-emotional competencies and to promote a sense of collective efficacy and shared purpose among staff.

Execution then shifts to providing students with consistent opportunities for high-quality social and emotional learning, beginning with the adoption of SEL standards and guidelines. Based on those standards, the district adopts and adapts an evidence-based program or programs and pursues ways to integrate SEL into academic instruction.

This phase entails alignment within the organization so that discipline policies and systems of student support provide a consistent and developmentally appropriate approach across departments and schools. This phase also involves strategies for partnering with families, out-of-school-time organizations, and community organizations so that there is a coherent and cohesive approach to the development of social and emotional competencies across the contexts of children's lives.

The last phase focuses on fostering continuous improvement so that problems of practice and inadequacies in execution can be identified and addressed. Utilizing the progress monitoring tools set out in the plan, systems are put in place for staff and administrators to reflect on student outcomes and implementation data compared with annual SEL goals and then to develop ongoing improvements to action plans, implementation strategies, and professional capacity building.

Organize, execute, and improve aren't necessarily distinct phases but overlapping cycles that continuously build over time as districts deepen and extend their efforts. Mahoney and colleagues argue that these practices provide the essence of a systemic approach to SEL implementation.

> The process at each setting begins with four coordinated sets of practices to establish EBPs [evidence-based practices] for children and adults: (a) Build foundational support and plan by establishing SEL teams, engaging stakeholders broadly, fostering awareness, and developing a shared vision; (b) Strengthen adult SEL competencies and capacity by cultivating a community of adults who engage in their own SEL, build trusting relationships, and collaborate to promote and consistently model SEL throughout the school; (c) Promote SEL for students by developing a coordinated approach across the school, classrooms, homes, and communities; and (d) Practice continuous improvement by establishing an ongoing process to collect and use implementation and outcome data to inform decisions and drive improvements. (Mahoney et al., 2018, p. 3)

Building upon the CASEL framework, Wright and her colleagues apply the Getting To Outcomes (GTO) approach to the implementation of SEL programs. They indicate that "GTO is a systematic process that can be used to support schools in selecting, implementing, and evaluating school-based programs that meet their individual needs and resources" (Wright et al., 2016, p. 500).

Through the use of ten framing questions that parallel and expand upon CASEL's framework, GTO's theoretical construct can readily be applied to reaching desired SEL-related outcomes. GTO asks the practitioner to consider the following:

- *Needs and Resources*: What are the underlying needs and conditions in the community (district/school)?
- *Goals*: What are the goals, target populations, and objectives (i.e., desired outcomes)?
- *Best Practices*: Which evidence-based models and best practice programs can be useful in reaching the goals?
- *Fit*: What actions need to be taken so that the selected program "fits" the community context?
- *Capacities*: What organizational capacities are needed to implement the plan?
- *Plan*: What is the plan for this program?
- *Implementation and Process Evaluation*: How will the quality of program implementation be monitored and assessed?
- *Outcome Evaluation*: How well did the program work?
- *CQI*: How will continuous quality improvement strategies be incorporated?
- *Sustainability*: If the program is successful, how will it be sustained? (Wright et al., 2016, p. 501)

AASA takes an approach similar to Wright's. In their handbook for district leaders, *Leading Social-Emotional Learning in Districts and Schools*, Dan Domenech and his colleagues at AASA provide a ten-point strategic planning matrix to support the SEL implementation process. Here are the ten framing questions for this matrix:

- Has your district established your mission, vision, and core values for SEL?
- Does your district reinforce ethics and professional norms that promote SEL?
- Do educators in your district understand the role of SEL in promoting equity and cultural responsiveness?
- Has your district intentionally and consistently integrated SEL into its curriculum, instruction, and assessment processes?
- To what extent does your district promote a community of caring and support for students through SEL?
- To what extent has your district ensured the SEL professional capacity of its school personnel?
- To what extent has your district integrated SEL into the professional community for teachers and staff?

- Does your district reinforce SEL via meaningful engagement of families and community?
- Is there evidence of the role of SEL in school and district operations and management?
- To what extent is SEL a catalyst for school improvement and district transformation? (Domenech et al., 2022, pp. 196–99)

TAKING SEL TO SCALE

It's helpful to have these systemic planning frameworks and organizing questions as background to better prepare for moving forward with implementation. However, implementation is often much messier, less orderly, and more complex than the frameworks would make it seem. Implementation theory only goes so far. In practice, the logical progression is often interrupted by multiple, competing agendas and by both the particular characteristics of the school district and the personalities of the individuals who will lead and implement the program.

Fortunately, there is research in the area of implementation of SEL programming that provides some insights into effective implementation strategies. Although most SEL research and related program evaluation have focused on whether particular SEL programs are supported by evidence of outcomes for students, a number of studies have focused instead on what enables a district to be more effective in its implementation of SEL programming.

In 2011, CASEL launched an initiative to attempt to systemically scale SEL in urban districts. Titled the Collaborating Districts Initiative or CDI, it initially involved three districts (Anchorage, Austin, and Cleveland), expanding to eight (Chicago, Nashville, Oakland, Sacramento, and Washoe County, Nevada) the following year.

The CDI has continued to grow, involving twenty districts in 2022. The initiative was supported by the Novo Foundation and the Einhorn Family Charitable Trust with $250,000 going to each of the eight districts for up to six years. The initiative allowed CASEL to support the districts' implementation efforts by helping them develop an SEL vision and long-term plan, conduct a needs and resources assessment, provide professional learning opportunities for staff, develop SEL learning standards, adopt and implement evidence-based programs, align SEL with other district activities, and monitor the implementation process.

Large urban districts are an implementation challenge for any adoption but, with CASEL's assistance, the CDI districts were largely successful in their implementation and scaling of SEL. The districts were able to cultivate commitment for SEL implementation, identify needs and resources to support implementation, establish SEL programming districtwide, and put in place a continuous improvement system to advance implementation over time.

Several evaluation studies were done, primarily by researchers from the American Institute of Research (AIR), to learn about the degree of implementation, the strategies for effective scaling of SEL, and the impact on student outcomes (Kendziora and Osher, 2016; Kendziora and Yoder, 2016; Schwartz et al., 2022). In terms of student outcomes, the CDI produced some positive trends in social and emotional, academic, and behavioral outcomes within the first five years of the initiative, particularly at the elementary level. The results showed that the initiative also improved school climate. In addition, the evaluation studies found that these districts were able to sustain, deepen, and broaden their commitment to SEL as well as strengthen their support for implementation. The districts made these gains in spite of periods of fiscal constraint and changes in leadership.

The initiative provided a number of lessons about implementation. Chief among them are that context is important and that districts followed different pathways toward the integration of SEL. Each district began at a different place and charted a different course based on its needs and resources. Additionally, the evaluation results indicated that district-level commitment and implementation enhanced the ability of schools to further their SEL efforts. As Greenberg and his colleagues found in their studies of implementation, when individual teachers and schools implement SEL strategies and programs, their efforts tend to be fragmented, lack coordination and systemic supports, and generally be insufficient to produce significant impact on students or sustainability over time (Greenberg et al., 2003).

Systemic implementation is best advanced and sustained at a district level by virtue of the district's decision-making and funding authority around curricula, instruction, and professional development (Kendziora and Osher, 2016). This systemic implementation is most effective when efforts to promote SEL are aligned with other district initiatives and the district's core functions, such as curriculum and instruction, student services, human resources, and financial planning.

CASEL's ten-year reflection on the CDI identifies the following six elements that support sustained and systemic implementation:

- Leaders model, cultivate, and elevate a shared vision for SEL.
- Core district priorities connect SEL to all departments and individuals, so everyone is invested.
- Schools have resources and pathways to guide SEL implementation, as well as room to innovate and customize SEL for their communities.
- SEL informs and shapes adult learning and staff culture and climate.
- Students, families, and communities are co-creators of the SEL vision, plans, and practices.
- External and internal communities of practice strengthen implementation. (CASEL, 2021, p. 4)

In addition, the participating CDI districts reported the importance of building the internal capacity for intensive coaching for schools and teachers. The districts also reported that strengthening adult SEL capabilities needed to be an earlier implementation priority. Many districts assume that teachers, by their very disposition, are prepared to serve as effective social and emotional role models and to foster SEL. That is not necessarily the case (Oliveira et al., 2021). The work on adult SEL development and depth of understanding of SEL practices is vital to effective implementation.

The EASEL Lab at the Harvard Graduate School of Education reviewed the research on SEL program implementation in its evaluation of secondary SEL programs. The lab found that it wasn't sufficient to simply select a strong, evidence-based program and put that program in place. Effective implementation was key to the success of any program (Jones et al., 2022).

The EASEL Lab team identified five conditions that support successful implementation:

- Allot the time required to implement the program sufficiently and effectively.
- Extend SEL beyond the classroom by providing opportunities to apply and transfer SEL skills and strategies.

- Ensure sufficient staff support and training.
- Facilitate program ownership and buy-in with staff, students, and families.
- Use data to guide decisions. (Jones et al., 2022, pp. 36–39)

District-based work relative to SEL implementation has drawn considerable investigatory attention over the past twenty years. As illustrated in both this section and the previous one, CASEL, AASA, and a number of researchers have independently arrived at findings that reveal significant overlap in effective approaches. This fact should give confidence to practitioners that the path described in these last two sections has a strong likelihood of supporting success at the school and district levels.

At the same time, while these conditions support implementation, they may still be insufficient to achieve depth in SEL practice. In fact, as the next section explains, there is much more to scaling implementation than simply changing structures and procedures.

DEPTH VS. SCALE

As Cynthia Coburn (2003) points out in her review of the research on the Child Development Project, "to be 'at scale,' reforms must effect deep and consequential change in classroom practice" (p. 4). Deep change involves altering "teachers' beliefs, norms of social interaction, and pedagogical principles as enacted in the curriculum" (p. 4).

Coburn (2003) further argues that effective scaling of any implementation has the following four requirements. First, it requires a depth of teacher knowledge and belief in the change that is reflected in daily classroom pedagogy and practice. In implementing SEL, it means understanding not only the skills that need to be fostered in young people, but how the culture and climate of the classroom, the social interaction between the teacher and students and among students, and the content and design of instruction all influence that development.

For some, says Coburn, scaling requires a significant shift in beliefs about teaching and classroom management as well as the ability to put those new beliefs into practical application in the classroom. Therefore, fostering and measuring change necessitates paying explicit attention to teachers' beliefs, norms, and pedagogical principles.

Second, according to Coburn's review of the research, going to scale is only meaningful when an intervention, new practice, or innovation is sustainable over time in the face of the realities of everyday district operations—competing priorities, changes in leadership, and financial constraints. She found that externally developed programs and practices adopted by a district are particularly vulnerable to these realities.

Coburn indicates that "teachers are better able to sustain change when there are mechanisms in place at multiple levels of the system to support their efforts" (2003, p. 6). These mechanisms include a supportive professional community of colleagues in the school who can reinforce changes and provide continuing opportunities to learn, as well as strong professional learning and coaching programs, support from school and district leaders, and alignment with district policies.

According to Coburn's analysis, a third factor in moving to scale with a change is spread, but not just in the typical sense of involving more classrooms and schools. Moving to scale does mean the spread of the underlying beliefs, norms, and principles of the change to other sites, but it also means the embodiment of those concepts in district policies and routines. In fact, district culture and district office expertise themselves become strategic sites for the spread. Demonstrated expertise in SEL among district leaders is an essential moving force in successful implementation.

The final factor in scaling for depth of implementation, observes Coburn, is a shift in reform ownership, in which the authority for the reform is held by the district, school leadership, and teachers. One of the essential strategies for scaling implementation is creating the conditions to shift authority from external sources to those involved in executing the change. Internal ownership enables the change to be self-regenerating.

This shift involves more than "teacher buy-in." It requires the development of commitments and capabilities on the part of teachers and administrators in order to take on sustaining the reform. It means developing the capacity for internally led professional learning systems through teacher leaders and coaches, professional communities of practice, and designated administrative leadership. Ownership at a district level is reflected in the policy and funding supports structurally and strategically built in to ensure continuity and growth. Reform-centered knowledge and decision-making are essential at the classroom, school, and district levels in order for ownership of the reform to be sustained over time.

In essence, our conceptualization of implementation has to consider not only how widely a strategy or change is used, but the depth of that practice. For SEL, depth of implementation is evidenced by multiple dimensions of teacher and school practice.

These dimensions include instructional design providing students with opportunities to interact in ways that embody the social skills being taught; the norms and culture of the classroom and school that reflect and represent a sense of community exemplified by connectedness, engagement, and shared responsibility; the professional culture among adults and the support systems for professional growth; and the district office's depth of knowledge and administrative support structures that ensure continuity and sustainability in support of SEL. Depth, spread, ownership, and sustainability constitute key implementation targets and a framework around which to organize implementation strategies (Coburn, 2003).

RESEARCH TAKEAWAYS

What can we take away from this research to support implementation of SEL? Some important findings rise to the top. Implementing SEL at a district level in a coordinated effort offers stronger support and more impactful and sustainable results than leaving it up to individual teachers and schools. However, there is no one cookie-cutter implementation plan. Each district has its own set of conditions that frame its entry points to implementation as well as the design and direction of its plans. The systemic implementation frameworks may serve as reference points when planning implementation, but each district must set its own course based on its unique history, needs, and resources.

Regardless of the diversity of starting points and approaches among districts, consistent support from district and school leadership in terms of commitment to SEL, along with the resources and policy structures that are put in place, are essential to the success of implementation. This leadership commitment involves support not only for implementing a specific SEL program or process, but for ensuring alignment with other district programs—as well as integration into such administrative departments as human resources, student services, and finance.

Finally, and probably most significant of all, the depth of adults' knowledge and understanding matters. The systems put in place for in-depth and continuing professional growth are instrumental in moving from initial stages of implementation to meaningful long-term benefit for both students and adults.

These elements of quality implementation plainly reveal themselves in the case studies presented in the coming chapters, as districts from six different parts of the country share how they applied the *why*, *what*, and *how* of SEL. In addition, as ethnographic portraits of districts' boots-on-the-ground experience, the case studies also portray the emergence of other key aspects of SEL implementation, offering insights into strategies that may work well for your district, plus how to address or avoid unanticipated obstacles.

Chapter 4

Striving for Deep and Transformational Learning

Virginia Beach City Public Schools (Virginia)

The Virginia Beach City Public Schools' (VBCPS) approach to social-emotional learning embodies the very spirit of social-emotional learning, that is, a concern for building a caring sense of community in classrooms and meaningful connections among adults and students. Superintendent Aaron Spence, who has been leading the Virginia Beach City division (Virginia uses the term "division" rather than "school district") for nine years, identifies the target of this work as all students feeling that they belong and that they are known, cared about, and loved.

The division's leaders—starting with the superintendent, his cabinet, and the professional learning specialist leading their SEL work—strive not only for implementation of effective practices but for a depth of understanding among administrators, faculty, and parents about what SEL is and how SEL practices can have a beneficial impact on teaching, classroom climate, and student learning. For division leaders, SEL represents the foundational support system for effective learning.

VBCPS is the fourth-largest school division in Virginia, serving nearly 64,000 students pre-K to grade 12 in fifty-six elementary schools, fifteen middle schools, twelve high schools and a number of secondary/post-secondary specialty centers. The community is a blend of farmland, urban core, resort area, and suburban development.

Four major military bases are located within the city boundaries, and approximately 20 percent of students are military-connected. The division's student population is highly diverse with 23 percent African American, 46 percent Caucasian, 13 percent Hispanic/Latino, 7 percent Asian, and 11 percent multiracial. Forty-four percent of students qualify as economically disadvantaged.

It is a powerful statement for an urban division the size of VBCPS to make such a strong commitment to SEL, and a lot of the credit for that goes to the superintendent. Aaron Spence grew up in Virginia Beach and graduated from one of the area's high schools. As a "hometown guy," he understands the history of the community and the nuances of the division's constituents, bringing to every situation a high level of credibility. His public recognition of the value of SEL has played a significant role in its acceptance by staff and families.

Given its size and diversity, VBCPS also has become a strong voice of support for SEL on the national stage, joining AASA's SEL Cohort and hosting a site visit so that other school districts can learn from their approach and their strategies. The division's SEL vision statement reads, "Each day students and adults learn about, develop and openly practice their social-emotional skills in a safe and equitable environment that prioritizes the well-being of individuals and the collective community." And the division's statement of core beliefs about SEL drives home the fundamental importance given to it:

- SEL begins with creating a safe environment for learning.
- SEL is focused on the well-being of children and staff.
- Belonging and inclusion are essential for achievement.
- SEL solidifies the connection kids have to school and the people in it.

The priority given to SEL is also deeply embedded in the division's vision, strategic plan, and priorities. VBCPS's Graduate Profile represents its vision for students and outlines eight characteristics the division wishes to cultivate in students. The Graduate Profile specifically identifies the characteristics of balance, resiliency, and personal and social responsibility as three of the eight characteristics that require social-emotional learning. Those characteristics are also embodied in the division's Compass to 2025 Strategic Framework, adopted in 2020.

The division's second strategic goal is student well-being, and the target is to "create an inclusive learning environment that supports the physical and mental health of all students and strengthens the social-emotional skills they need to become balanced, resilient learners who are personally and socially responsible."

Compass to 2025 also identifies a number of specific strategies for reaching the goal of student well-being through the integration of SEL across the division, including the following:

- Provide a safe, welcoming, and inclusive learning environment that is conducive to student learning.
- More deeply integrate social-emotional learning (SEL) into the pre-K to grade 12 curriculum.
- Use responsive practices such as morning meetings and student advisories to support SEL.
- Engage in culturally responsive practices at the classroom, school, and division levels.
- Implement procedures to systematically evaluate behavioral and mental health needs and provide programs and services to meet identified needs.
- Continue to use Student Response Teams (SRTs) and the Positive Behavioral Interventions and Supports (PBIS) framework to provide social, emotional, and behavioral support to students.

The Graduate Profile, Compass to 2025 strategic plan, and other documents are all public-facing with the intent of communicating to staff, parents, and the community at large the critical importance of SEL for moving the district and student learning forward.

Reflecting its seriousness about implementing SEL effectively, the division established a Social-Emotional Learning Implementation Team (SEL-IT), under the auspices of chief academic officer Dr. Kipp Rogers, with more than forty members crossing multiple disciplines and departments. Superintendent Spence convened this broad team to guide the implementation of SEL in order to "have a group of people who think about it every day with the intent of baking it into the culture of the division."

The SEL programming that the division has implemented to support this goal, plus the professional development provided to build staff capacity to implement it effectively, reflect an approach that places authentic relationships and authentic, student-centered learning at the forefront of the division's efforts. In a presentation to a group of administrators from school districts interested in VBCPS's SEL programming, division leadership framed their approach with the following quote from a leader with Learning Forward, an organization focused on professional learning in education:

> Deep learning, often called transformational learning, occurs at the level of beliefs, values, and motivation rather than only at the level of knowledge and skills. Transformational learning is long-term and results in behavioral changes; it is deep change that occurs at the core of the learner. (Joellen Killion, Senior Advisor, Learning Forward)

It is this deep, transformational learning that division leaders are pursuing with the goal of building staff capacity for facilitating social-emotional learning in students. Their design is to use agile strategic planning to enable nimble, just-in-time adjustments to best move the plan forward, coupled with an "activation curve" from consulting firm XPlane to move people's support from hearing and learning about SEL to believing in it to living it through internalization, passionate advocacy, and cultural embeddedness.

The division is not pursuing compliance with a division directive, but rather seeks deep understanding and ownership of the meaning, importance, and vitality of SEL practice.

THE EVOLUTION OF SEL IN VIRGINIA BEACH

Although the division's early work on social-emotional development began around 2007 with a focus on twenty-first-century skills such as listening, collaboration, communication, and social responsibility, it wasn't until the Compass to 2020 Strategic Framework was adopted in 2015 that SEL was named as a strategic action. Compass to 2020 set a goal of promoting social-emotional development, stating that "all students will benefit from an educational experience that fosters their social and emotional development."

The first years of SEL efforts involved defining what the term meant organizationally and beginning to explore programs that met that definition. The division eventually adopted CASEL's definition from 2018 (since updated) that SEL is "formally defined as the process through which children and adults acquire and effectively apply the knowledge, attitudes, and skills necessary to understand and manage emotions, set and achieve positive goals, feel and show empathy for others, establish and maintain positive relationships, and make responsible decisions."

In a site-based division such as VBCPS, schools can make their individual choice to pursue programs that strive to achieve the larger goals set by the division. In the early years of the division's SEL efforts, elementary schools began exploring two programs that placed less emphasis on direct instruction in social skills and more emphasis on supporting the teacher in creating a classroom climate and culture that enabled students to learn the skills by living them in their daily life in the classroom.

Some schools began using Responsive Classroom from the Center for Responsive Schools, while others explored the Caring School Community program out of the Center for the Collaborative Classroom. As elementary schools communicated with each other about these programs, they began leaning toward Responsive Classroom and requesting professional learning supports for Responsive Classroom practices. The Responsive Classroom program was more attractive at the elementary and middle school levels largely because it was more closely aligned with the division's teaching standard relative to the learning environment.

Nationally, there is a dearth of SEL programs for the secondary level, particularly for high schools. Although some Virginia Beach City middle schools began exploring Responsive Classroom's middle school program, the high schools chose to prioritize opportunities for community building.

An advisory program has been evolving for several years and, prior to the pandemic, all high schools were utilizing a One Lunch model. This extended, fifty-minute lunch enables all students to eat at the same time rather than in multiple short periods of twenty to thirty minutes. The One Lunch model affords opportunities for students to gather together as a school, in addition to time to meet with teachers during office hours, attend club meetings, get support from the Peer Tutoring Center, and foster a culture of inclusivity through a variety of activities, such as open gym, games, and book clubs.

RESPONSIVE TEACHING PRACTICES

Developed in 1981, Responsive Classroom was one of the earliest and most well-developed of the K–8 social-emotional learning programs. To support school districts and schools in implementing the program, the Center for Responsive Schools provides a wide variety of books on various elements of the program, in addition to an in-depth, multilevel, professional development series.

Responsive Classroom offers three levels of professional development that address not only SEL practices, but the very nature of the classroom environment. The program is distinct among SEL programs for its focus on creating classroom and instructional environments that nurture students' social-emotional growth, rather than teaching students specific social skills through skills-based lessons. In fact, it wasn't until 2021 that the center released a skills-based social development program, titled Fly Five, to accompany its Responsive Classroom program.

In essence, Responsive Classroom is an approach to teaching. The program provides teachers with the instructional and classroom management strategies and training to create a sense of community and respect in the classroom. The goal is to foster classroom environments where students get to know and care about each other and where adults refine their practices and language to model and support the ways they wish students to act.

The focus on creating a caring classroom community is central to students' learning that their actions have an impact on others and can make a difference that benefits others and the classroom as a whole. Within this supportive environment, students are better able to take learning risks and learn from their mistakes, and thereby feel more confident in taking the next steps in their learning. Because most of the Responsive Classroom practices are woven into the daily routines, learning activities, and flow of the classroom, they do not stand out as a separate unit of study but rather become a way of life in the classroom. In this way, students live their way into developing their social and emotional skills.

Responsive Classroom is a CASEL SELect Program; numerous evaluation studies have shown that it helps students develop social skills and also improve academically (Rimm-Kaufman & Chiu, 2007;

Rimm-Kaufman et al., 2007). For example, the Ecological Approaches to Social Emotional Learning (EASEL) Laboratory of the Harvard Graduate School of Education found that Responsive Classroom not only focuses on the development of prosocial and cooperation skills, but also provides support for such cognitive growth areas such as attention control, working memory and planning skills, inhibitory control, cognitive flexibility, and critical thinking (Jones et al., 2021, p. 337).

Responsive Classroom aligns well with VBCPS's focus on deep, transformational learning as well as with its goal of promoting student-centered instruction. As an approach to teaching, Responsive Classroom has set forth a number of guiding principles (Responsive Classroom, n.d.), two of which the division has specifically adopted as core beliefs within its own design of a responsive teaching logic model:

- Teaching social and emotional skills is as important as teaching academic content.
- How we teach is as important as what we teach.

In addition, the division added three more core beliefs:

- Teaching and learning are social endeavors.
- Social and emotional learning is best nurtured in supportive relationships.
- Responsive Classroom practices are interdependent and most impactful when used together.

The division's purpose in implementing Responsive Classroom, as articulated in the original program's Responsive Teaching Logic Model, is to "transform the culture of classrooms and schools in VBCPS so that students experience a sense of belonging and thrive socially, emotionally, and academically." At the elementary level, the division has focused on four specific areas of developmentally responsive teaching.

The first is the building of an inclusive, caring community through morning meetings and closing circles. Each day's morning meeting lasts approximately twenty minutes and involves several components. As students enter the classroom, they are greeted by a morning message from the teacher about the day ahead, as well as a quick, do-now, warm-up activity. The teacher then gathers the students in a circle and engages them in greeting each other by name, varying the greeting activity from day to day. Next, there is a sharing activity in which a number of students each day are able to share something that is important to them or an important event in their lives while other students listen empathetically and ask clarifying questions.

Finally, the teacher engages everyone in a brief, lively activity to promote both group cohesion and fun. This activity can also be related to the academic skills students will learn or practice later that day. Morning meeting closes with the teacher or a student reading the morning message. These activities engage all students, encourage students to know and care about each other, and set a positive tone for the day.

Just as it is valuable for students to start each day constructively, it's important for them to bring it to a meaningful closure. At the end of the day students gather in a closing circle and are asked by the teacher to reflect on such questions as "What is one thing you learned today that you did not know?" or "What is one thing that you feel you did well today?" or "What is one way you saw someone help someone else today?" Students voice their reflections on the day and hear their peers' thoughts in turn. The closing circle enables students to leave school feeling calmer and with a sense of resolution and community.

A second area of responsive teaching VBCPS has focused on is teacher language. Teacher language and tone can have a powerful influence on the culture of the classroom. Sarcasm, judgmental comments both positive and negative, threats, labeling, and even tone of voice can undermine the classroom culture the teacher is trying to create and the very social skills that students are trying to learn. Accordingly, the division is helping teachers focus on language that genuinely acknowledges students' work and behavior, using nonjudgmental feedback that is both validating and constructive. The emphasis on teacher language also includes helping teachers deal with challenging situations in a calm and constructive manner.

VBCPS's third area of focus has been integrating social-emotional learning strategies into academic instruction through three signature practices that support productive social engagement and social learning in the classroom. These are the three signature practices:

- an inclusive opening
- engaging learning strategies
- an intentional closing

These interactive, purposeful, instructional activities are designed to actively engage students as they practice social skills in their routine classroom pursuits. The division provides a resource bank of suggested ways to implement each of these signature strategies so that teachers have ready examples to use in their classrooms. Identifying the key practices that teachers should focus on makes the integration of these student-centered strategies more manageable.

The fourth area of focus in the division's approach to responsive teaching is interactive modeling, in which the teacher models a behavior or skill that students are expected to learn—without describing it—and then asks students what they observed. The behavior can be one that occurs in the course of a typical school day, such as carrying scissors, using the pencil sharpener, or pushing a chair into the table. After they share, the students model it for each other and again discuss what they noticed. This gives the students an opportunity to practice it, reflect on it, and receive feedback, all the while interacting with peers and the teacher.

The four focus areas are designed to foster caring classroom communities in which every student feels a sense of belonging and connection to others. Teaching in these classrooms is transformative by providing the safety and support students require to learn best.

Responsive Classroom utilizes similar practices at the middle school level with an emphasis on a Responsive Advisory period to build a sense of community among students. The division has just begun working with middle schools to learn about this approach to social-emotional learning.

With the adoption of Compass to 2020, efforts to personalize learning and increase engagement were a focus at all levels. At the high school level, these efforts have developed into a high school redesign plan. The division already provides students with ways they can pursue their interests through career academies and extracurricular activities. The high school redesign plan is intended to support the three student-focused goals in the division's strategic framework—student ownership, student well-being, and educational excellence.

To realize those goals, the redesign focuses on enabling students to participate in real-world learning experiences, to develop meaningful plans for postsecondary pursuits, and to produce student-curated works of substance and engage in a signature experience. SEL is a foundational component of high school redesign, along with equity and innovation. The components of redesign prioritize engagement, personalization, authenticity, and ownership, and all areas are viewed through the lens of equity, social-emotional learning, and innovation.

High school faculty are pursuing strategies such as faculty outreach to students and collaborative learning experiences to ensure that all students feel known and valued. While the redesign is still in its early stages, many of the high schools have adopted practices in which faculty are focused on getting to know their students as individuals with interests, goals, and concerns beyond the classroom.

PURSUING DEPTH OF IMPLEMENTATION

Reflective of the deep learning philosophy adopted by its professional growth and innovation (PGI) specialists and the administrative team in general, the division placed its emphasis on developing professional capacity—not only to implement specific programs but to actually lead the initial and ongoing implementation of those programs.

One of the first efforts to ensure depth was to convene a team of key stakeholders to help move the initiative forward. In order to engage all departments within the division, the Social-Emotional Learning Implementation Team (SEL-IT) brought together forty individuals drawn from every area that had some relationship to SEL. It included central office administrators, principals, specialists, and teachers.

Cochaired by Angelyn Nichols, a PGI professional learning specialist, and Robert Jamison, coordinator of school counseling services, the SEL-IT divided itself into work teams in such areas as SEL curriculum, strategic planning, SEL survey, student voice and leadership, trauma sensitivity, adult well-being, and responsive practices. The full team meets every eight weeks, while project leads for each of the work teams meet every three to four weeks. This structure has ensured intra-division awareness and involvement in the planning and development of SEL implementation.

Beyond broad investment in the implementation of SEL, the SEL-IT has promoted alignment across departments. For example, tensions often exist between the classroom and school practices that are advocated by Positive Behavioral Interventions and Support (PBIS) programs, which tend to focus on extrinsic rewards to promote positive behavior, and community-building programs such as Responsive Classroom, which focus on intrinsic meaning and relationships to support prosocial behavior. In VBCPS, the leaders of SEL and PBIS have worked together to create an alignment guide around goals, guidelines, language, and behavior-specific responses so that the two efforts are mutually supportive.

VBCPS's PBIS team has moved to focus on student voice and agency, engaging students in dialogue about behavior expectations and effective intervention strategies similar to the norm-setting conversations that are part of the Responsive Classroom program. This kind of intentional and thoughtful alignment is also emerging in the division's work on trauma-sensitive supports and adult well-being.

Equally significant is a strategic focus on multiple avenues of professional development to ensure that teachers and administrators develop the skills and approaches necessary to implement SEL well in schools and classrooms. For elementary teachers, the division provides in-depth, week-long training in Responsive Classroom practices. This training has reached more than four hundred teachers and administrators over the past three years.

For those who are interested, the division also makes the second—or advanced—level of week-long Responsive Classroom training available. In addition, some teachers and specialists are being supported in taking the third level of training from Responsive Classroom to become certified Responsive Classroom trainers so that this training can be brought in-house and sustained well into the future. The division has titled this effort their Responsive Classroom Academy, and some schools are engaging their entire faculty in participating in the trainings.

The professional growth and innovation team supports teachers enrolled in the academy with on-going professional learning through the school year. Over the 2021–2022 school year, the academy engaged sixty teachers from eighteen schools at the elementary level and thirty teachers from six schools at the secondary level. At the same time, eighteen teachers drawn from thirteen schools were involved in the advanced-level training. The PGI team is also planning to offer training for bus drivers, nutrition services staff, security officers, and nurses so that all staff in the schools are able to understand and apply a responsive approach in their interactions with students.

In addition, the PGI team provides a classroom learning series composed of a three-part, self-paced, asynchronous course open to all staff to introduce the essentials of classroom SEL. For those who are interested in collaborating with colleagues to dive more deeply into SEL practices, the PGI team convenes SEL communities of practice that meet every six weeks and focus on the five core SEL competencies.

The PGI team also developed an SEL Integration Fellows program to support a cohort of teachers who want to more deeply integrate SEL into their classrooms. With the support of Angelyn Nichols, the PGI professional learning specialist who leads the initiative, the fellows will go through cycles of reflection and feedback in a year of professional learning. These individuals will be prepared to open their classrooms as model classrooms for other teachers to observe. The PGI team has also put in place a classroom specialization in SEL in which teachers can earn a micro-credential for their mastery of integrating SEL into their classrooms.

In essence, the division supports numerous and varied training opportunities for staff members to delve more deeply in order to develop mastery in SEL. The commitment of the division is to build a depth of capacity among staff so that the skills they learn can be effectively applied in the classroom not only today but for the foreseeable future.

COMMUNICATING THE MEANING OF SEL

In the fall of 2021, public controversies emerged in numerous states, including Virginia, over the teaching of critical race theory (CRT) in schools. Although there was no indication that critical race theory was taught in VBCPS or in most other public schools, the controversy bled over to the teaching of social-emotional learning. As the division prepared its own response to the public, there was a realization that it needed to provide clarity in the meaning and purpose of SEL, not only for the public but for the faculty and staff.

Working with the communications department, professional learning specialist Angelyn Nichols and other members of the SEL-IT developed a "message map" that targeted three essential talking points about the value of SEL in VBCPS classrooms:

- SEL helps young people develop the skills they need to succeed in school and life.
- SEL is focused on creating a safe and inclusive learning environment for all students.
- SEL is about the well-being of young people.

Each point was supported by a bulleted list of explanations and evidence. Along with the message map, the division developed a document that included a definition of SEL, a delineation of the skills embodied in each of the five SEL core competencies, and four specific strategies for supporting social-emotional development in schools:

- Provide a safe, welcoming, and equitable learning environment.
- Use social-emotional learning strategies that are embedded within the Teaching and Learning Framework.
- Enhance student engagement in classroom, school, and community activities.
- Establish strong, tiered levels of support to respond to student needs.

These documents were shared with faculty, parents, and the community to ensure that there was clarity around what SEL is, why it's important, and the ways it shows up in classrooms and schools. To more fully understand perceptions of staff around SEL, Angelyn Nichols led a listening tour in which she interviewed teachers and instructional coaches. Realizing that many staff members had divergent definitions of the meaning and practice of SEL, communication became a central strategy for the SEL-IT.

The result has been a more consistent understanding about SEL among staff and the community at large. With the superintendent continually explaining that SEL is laying a foundation of belonging and care, support for and acceptance of SEL has remained strong in the division despite state and national controversies.

DYNAMIC USE OF FORMATIVE SEL DATA

Receiving and examining feedback are essential for refining practice, and VBCPS is taking significant steps on an ongoing basis to provide that information to schools. First, the division has engaged Panorama Education to survey students about their own skill development in the SEL competencies, using four scales that reflect students' sense of belonging and support (teacher-student relationships, sense of belonging, engagement, and school safety) and four SEL skill areas that support well-being (supportive relationships, social awareness, self-efficacy, and emotional regulation).

Typically, these data are provided to the schools without student-specific information and are reviewed by the schools' data teams in order to establish goals and track progress. However, for twenty-one schools, the division is piloting the use of student-identifiable data so that the school staff can provide specific strategies based on grade, classroom, and student information. The overall goal is to use the data to reflect on the school environment, teacher support, and effectiveness of SEL practices, and to make adjustments that better address students' perceptions and needs.

The concern in providing student-identifiable data is that it may shift the focus to viewing the student as the problem rather than enabling staff to see the practices and environment within the classroom or school as the issue that should be addressed. This pilot effort will strive to sustain the goal of reflection on the environment and couple it with a closer examination of the supports that particular students may need.

As a second means of pursuing data-based improvement, the PGI team has provided teachers and administrators with a number of learning walk protocols. These tools support both peer and administrative walk-throughs that can offer feedback to teachers and help highlight "look-for" practices. Each learning walk protocol focuses on a specific SEL practice, such as morning meeting, teacher language, or engaging academics, as well as such essential SEL components as building a supportive classroom environment, integrating SEL into academic instruction, and explicitly teaching SEL skills.

These protocols enable teachers in their professional learning communities and administrators in their daily walk-throughs to offer just-in-time feedback to teachers while deepening their own understanding of SEL. The protocols have become a core element in the professional growth opportunities provided as part of the division's SEL implementation.

Both the data teams' use of student survey data and the teachers' and administrators' use of the learning walk protocols promote the kind of deep reflection and professional growth the division is pursuing.

ACCESSIBLE RESOURCES

To better support teacher adoption of SEL and its signature practices, VBCPS has developed an extensive online resource bank called "the stockpile" that is accessible to anyone in the district at any stage of their SEL professional journey. Not only does the stockpile include basic information on the division's SEL framework and message maps, it also contains numerous videos on SEL instructional practices from CASEL and Edutopia, as well as district-created material. There are numerous examples of strategies teachers can use to provide inclusive openings, engaging learning strategies, and intentional closings.

Included in the stockpile are additional articles, action guides, and professional learning tools, such as a playbook for analyzing Panorama data. In addition, there are developmental targets and "I can" statements, delineated by grade span, that teachers and administrators can build into their instructional lesson planning.

INSIGHTS FROM IMPLEMENTATION

Supporting change and growth in a large, site-based school district is challenging. The central office serves as a guide and resource in hopes of providing sufficient direction and support to move student performance forward. In such a school system, leadership is an essential element of districtwide success. Fortunately, stable and effective leadership is one of the strengths of VBCPS and has helped produce significant advances in implementation of SEL practices.

Not only is Superintendent Spence a talented and courageous division leader, but his longevity through nine years has provided consistency and focus. He has been able to address controversies in a clear and calming manner, continually articulating the core purpose of SEL as enabling all students to feel cared about, known, and supported within a positive classroom and school environment. He has made it clear that he will shoulder the responsibility for public debates and board relations so that others can continue to do the critical work on the ground.

In addition, he has established an effective leadership structure for guiding SEL implementation. The broad-based nature of the SEL-IT makes a statement that SEL is owned by everyone. Assigning the co-facilitation of the SEL-IT to two very talented and experienced central office individuals, one representing teaching and professional learning and the other representing student services, ensures that SEL implementation is not perceived as something only for students with particular needs and instead is intimately connected with daily instruction and school culture for all students.

Assigning an individual from Professional Growth and Innovation to lead the SEL effort—Angelyn Nichols, who has taught at every level and served as an exemplary instructional coach—provides an experienced and knowledgeable point of contact for everyone and demonstrates the priority the division places on the work. Bringing a diverse group of division leaders together to support the effort has also resulted in collaboration and alignment across departments.

The superintendent has also ensured that there is a deep, division-wide commitment to the initiative by embedding it into plans and policies that not only guide the allocation of division resources but provide the core elements of school improvement planning. Building on Compass to 2020, the current Compass to 2025 Strategic Framework makes SEL a priority and specifies the actions the division and schools need to pursue in order to make progress in meeting the framework's goals.

The focus on communication has served both to alleviate controversy and build support. Developing a consistent, meaningful message about SEL provides the ground on which teachers, administrators, and parents can understand why the district values SEL and the essential learning experiences that students will have as a result. The refinement and dissemination of the message—the *why*, *what*, and *how* of SEL—was an astute move that recentered the SEL implementation work, moderated the controversies for most individuals, and built confidence that the work would continue to be supported as essential to achieving the division's goals.

Probably most significant in ensuring the long-running success of VBCPS in realizing SEL has been the division's pursuit of depth of understanding and implementation. Unfortunately, many SEL programs suffer from a lack of professional development, thinking that teachers can adopt practices with one- to two-hour trainings or online videos. Nothing could be further from the truth.

In contrast, VBCPS, with its weeklong professional development trainings and yearlong communities of practice and fellowships, has put in place structures that support the development of significant expertise to implement SEL well. The provision of multiple in-depth professional development opportunities, instructional coaching, and voluminous instructional resources takes staff from initial understanding to internalization and embedded practice. These efforts speak to the division's appreciation that once individuals reach that level of expert practice and personal investment in an approach or program, they will not abandon the expertise they have developed. It will become the natural heartbeat of the way they teach and lead.

In addition, the division—and the PGI team in particular—has prioritized the promotion of reflective practice that engages teachers in thoughtful refinement of their teaching practice. The data teams, communities of practice, instructional coaching, and learning walk protocols constitute strategies that promote teacher ownership and collegial collaboration. They serve to strengthen the foundation of SEL practice.

In essence, the district is pursuing wrap-around support for its implementation of SEL by providing clear leadership, extensive professional development opportunities, multiple reflection and feedback tools and processes, and a comprehensive set of supportive resources.

CONCLUSION

VBCPS's efforts have built a strong foundation for the success of SEL implementation, particularly at the elementary level. However, going deep sometimes means building from the ground up rather than mandating consistency and fidelity from the top. Although many of the division's elementary schools now provide exemplary SEL practices, others are just at the beginning or have yet to begin. The work at the middle and high school levels is also at an initial stage of development.

Going deep means that one has to be patient and know that consistency and fidelity take years to achieve.

Given that reality, the strategies that the division has utilized for moving forward—from agile strategic planning to in-depth professional development and from division-wide goal setting to investment in leadership targeted to support SEL—are providing a high level of investment and ownership among division and school leaders and teachers. That ownership and the internalization of the importance and vitality of SEL will enable the division to continue to build toward more effective levels of instructional practice, not only in the social-emotional arena but in the academic arena as well.

Chapter 5

Responding to Demographic Challenges

Marshalltown Community School District (Iowa)

Marshalltown is a community of twenty-eight thousand residents, located in the farmlands of central Iowa. While its economy has a strong focus on agriculture and farming, it is also the longtime home of some well-known companies in the advanced manufacturing sector. Once a flourishing and affluent area, Marshalltown has undergone dramatic demographic and economic changes over the past three decades. Although some of the advanced manufacturing companies have retained a sizable presence, globalization prompted others to move their headquarters out of Marshalltown and to build new plants in other areas of the country and the world. These moves resulted in a significant loss of professional-level jobs and wages, even as the town's population remained relatively stable.

Today, the largest local employer is a pork production plant, and Marshalltown has emerged as one of Iowa's most racially diverse and economically challenged communities. Of the district's 5,200 students, 72 percent qualify for free or reduced-price meal assistance, 69 percent are students of color, 33 percent do not speak English as their primary language (most speak Spanish), and the mobility rate is 20 percent. Almost all of the district's schools qualify for Title I support.

In addition to the challenges presented by the changing demographics and economic decline, the community has been hit by a series of environmental disasters. The school district first began working on systematic implementation of social-emotional learning during the spring of the 2017–2018 school year. An EF3 tornado struck that summer, devastating the downtown area and numerous homes in the community.

Then, in August of 2020, the community was inundated by a derecho—or land-based hurricane—that did even more damage to businesses and homes. Today, still reeling from the health and economic impacts of the COVID pandemic, the community has yet to recover from these two weather-related events; buildings in the downtown area and around the community still have gaping holes where walls and roofs once stood.

Beyond the devastating impact that these events have had on physical structures, the children in the community have experienced—and continue to experience—a great deal of disruption in their home and school lives, evidencing physical, behavioral, and mental health and trauma issues that teachers, counselors, and administrators in the district must face and attempt to address. Although the community came together as neighbors supporting neighbors, the strain of these events has left many families and children handicapped in their ability to manage their circumstances with any sense of normalcy.

THE EVOLUTION OF SEL PROGRAMMING

In small communities such as Marshalltown that have experienced traumatic events, social-emotional learning takes a different path than the one that large districts follow, and intensive efforts are required to provide multi-tiered systems of support (MTSS). Given the district's size and significant budget constraints, the few administrators in the central office are left to shoulder the responsibility of moving SEL forward as part of their already overwhelming workload.

Fortunately for Marshalltown, the district's leadership believes that children in the community, particularly at this point in time, need the support and healing that SEL offers. School and district administrators are strongly committed to developing effective programs that address students' needs. In fact, one of the primary reasons for the progress the district has made in its SEL efforts is the personal commitment of district leaders to take the time to learn about SEL in depth and to take an active leadership role in moving a strategic implementation plan forward.

In 2016, Dr. Theron Schutte returned to the district from which he had once graduated, newly appointed as Marshalltown's superintendent. Although the community had changed much since he donned a cap and gown in 1981, he brought with him a deep understanding of the community, its history, and its culture. As someone who is known to have been nurtured by this very community, he conveys a degree of credibility that complements his naturally soft-spoken and pragmatic style. As a result, he has experienced little resistance and, in fact, much support in moving SEL forward.

Marshalltown's director of special services, Matt Cretsinger, has assumed the day-to-day mantle of SEL implementation along with overseeing many other programs and services, including special education, 504 services, mental health community partnerships, school counseling, social work services, health and behavioral health services, pre-K programming for children with disabilities, and Medicaid services. A member of the district's leadership team since 2012, his longevity has provided a stability and consistency that have enabled SEL programming to expand and deepen over time.

In 2017, after a year of collaboration with the community on the development of a five-year strategic plan, the district's board of education approved a plan that encompasses SEL. To achieve the goal of improving the learning environment and enhancing the culture and climate for students, the district committed to "expand and enhance social, emotional, and behavioral supports at pre-K through 12."

To support this goal, two early initiatives laid a foundation for more significant SEL efforts. The first was the implementation of Positive Behavioral Interventions and Supports (PBIS). Administrators and teachers were initially trained in PBIS strategies in 2010. The district continues to use PBIS but has recently shifted away from using a token reward system for all but a small segment of students. The motivation for PBIS came from a sense that students needed a predictable environment in which expectations were clearly defined and consistently maintained in order for students to feel safe and become emotionally and behaviorally regulated.

Although PBIS is effective in creating a more consistent set of expectations for behaviors, the tension in its implementation is that it tends to promote compliance rather than building autonomy and intrinsic motivation. As Matt Cretsinger notes, "PBIS teaches routines, not skills." Skill development requires a less adult-directed system of supports through the creation of responsive communities in classrooms and schools and specific skill development curricula that have real-life application in the classroom.

The second foundational initiative focused less on students and more on how adults managed their interactions with students. Mr. Cretsinger heard a presentation by Stuart Ablon from Massachusetts General Hospital on the collaborative problem-solving (CPS) strategies he was using in his MGH practice (Ablon, 2018). After further research, Director Cretsinger proposed that Marshalltown begin the process of implementing the CPS approach in Marshalltown in accordance with the Think:Kids initiative directed by Dr. Ablon.

The district partnered with its regional education center, the Central Rivers Area Education Agency (CRAEA), to bring Dr. Ablon to Marshalltown to speak to the entire staff and the community. His presentation launched several years of district collaboration with CRAEA, including support for staff training in CPS.

The partnership with the area education agency was critical to helping the district move forward, not only with CPS but with the district's overall SEL planning, especially in its earliest stages. The district gave priority to CPS in its professional development programming and in its leadership support. In fact, to support the implementation of CPS more fully, Mr. Cretsinger is participating in a training program over the next three years to become an in-house CPS trainer.

COLLABORATIVE PROBLEM SOLVING

The research that Ablon and his colleagues at MGH have done reveals that adults, whether in school or at home, generally take the wrong approach to addressing challenging behaviors, and the systems of school and home discipline often accentuate rather than address problems. The conventional response to challenging behaviors assumes that the child is misbehaving because of attitude, lack of interest, obstinacy, will, and so forth. The child knows better but isn't acting accordingly, and the disobedience or dysregulation is a willful attempt to manipulate the situation. Based on that assumption, we exert adult control in order to manage the situation and administer punishment to teach the child a lesson.

Ablon argues that our assumptions are wrong and lead us to actions that only accentuate the behavior and undermine trust in adults. In the research on and treatment of significant behavioral issues, he and his colleagues found that the actions of the child are not based on will, but rather on a lack of skill in particular areas of development.

These areas include communication and language skills that enable the child to communicate the problems being experienced; emotional self-regulation and frustration tolerance skills that enable a child to think before acting; cognitive flexibility and adaptability skills that enable a child to see alternatives to patterns of behavior; attention and working memory skills that enable a child to problem-solve in difficult situations; and social thinking skills that enable a child to perceive the impact on others and know how to address social situations appropriately.

Delays in development may result from chronic stress and/or trauma that arrests brain development. However, rewards and punishments don't work to address lagging skills; only skill development can address them. And that skill development doesn't come from a boxed curriculum, but from the collaborative problem-solving dialogue that takes place in real situations.

The strategies for teaching these skills require a profound level of listening and empathy to hear what the child's behavior is telling us about personal feelings and concerns as well as the developmental lags that are getting in the way of the child's responding more appropriately. The strategies also require collaboration with the child in problem-solving dialogues that take the concerns of the child seriously in finding a solution. In fact, the dialogue begins with empathizing with the child to clarify what the problem is before sharing the adult concern about the behavior.

If a child is dysregulated, CPS begins with reflective listening and reassurance until the student is calm and regulated. Once the adult understands the issue from the child's perspective, the adult's concern can be expressed and both parties can collaboratively explore ways to address both the child's and the adult's concerns.

In essence, the CPS approach requires adults to suspend their immediate reactive response to acting-out children, listen to what children are telling them about how they feel and what they need, and find solutions that address the children's, not just the adults', concerns. In the process of the collaborative problem-solving dialogue with the adult, children begin to develop those skills that have been lagging in their development.

Ablon has found that children want to be successful and that "kids do well if they can." The challenge is that they lack the skills to do well. CPS is successful because it is based on collaboration rather than power and control. It focuses attention on understanding and support for skill development over time. And it fosters a trusting relationship in which children experience their concerns being taken seriously, and they feel supported in their developmental growth.

What is so instrumental about CPS as a foundation for social-emotional learning is that it shifts the focus away from blaming the child to focusing on the environment, past experiences, and other factors that may be creating issues in the child's development. It builds a more responsive environment and more trusting adult-child relationship. The professional development and ongoing coaching in CPS provide key supports for effective implementation of social-emotional learning practices.

THE DISTRICT IMPLEMENTATION PLAN

Although PBIS and CPS offer a strong foundation for supporting SEL programming, they are not sufficient in and of themselves to establish the social skill development and classroom and school culture that quality SEL programs can provide. Understanding that the district needed to take additional measures, an SEL steering committee was formed to delineate next steps and make decisions about program selection.

The committee comprises approximately a dozen people including central office administrators, principals, counselors, and teachers. Led by the director of special services, the steering committee established a vision statement for SEL: "The Marshalltown Community School District's vision for SEL is to actively promote social-emotional learning by providing high-quality teaching and learning experiences on social-emotional development."

The committee put in place universal screeners—the Social, Academic, and Emotional Behavioral Risk Screener (SAEBRS) as well as MySAEBRS—for data teams to use in assessing which areas needed better support. In addition, the counselors adopted the Positive Action guidance curriculum to deliver in classrooms. Marshalltown adopted Responsive Classroom at the elementary level and Capturing Kids' Hearts at the secondary level. The district provided one day of training in Responsive Classroom for all administrators and counselors and began supporting teachers in attending Responsive Classroom's week-long training.

Based on the committee's recommendation, in 2020–2021, the district's portion of monthly professional development days (the other half are school-based) were devoted to workshops on the State of Iowa's newly adopted social-emotional core competencies. These sessions were followed in 2021–2022 with sessions on building positive relationships, building classroom community, empathy development, and relationship and communication skills. The focus of these sessions was not only on what these competencies are but on what they mean for classroom practice.

While each of the six K–4 elementary schools and the grades 5–6 intermediate school have had some teachers participate in Responsive Classroom trainings, overall Anson Elementary has pursued the program most comprehensively and with a great deal of enthusiasm. Encouraged and supported by the principal and school counselor, all but one of Anson's teachers have participated in Responsive Classroom trainings.

They are using Responsive Classroom's "hopes and dreams" norm-setting process at the start of the year, morning and closing meetings, quiet times, and class meetings so that classes can problem-solve around issues and concerns. They have established a vertical cross-grade-level team to check on progress. Their focus is on building strong relationships and a sense of community, and the school is serving as a model for others in the district.

Following Anson's lead, a second elementary school has now trained its entire staff in Responsive Classroom. (Note: Responsive Classroom practices are described in detail in chapter 4.)

Founded by Flip Flippen in the early 1990s, Capturing Kids' Hearts seeks to create a positive environment in which students as well as the teacher take ownership of the culture of the classroom and the expectations that students have of each other. The school year begins with each class developing a "social contract" outlining how students wish to be treated by peers and adults, how students should treat others, and how conflicts should be resolved. The contract is signed by all students and the teacher in order to demonstrate everyone's commitment to these norms. This document becomes a reference point when a student is not following the contract and, through nonverbal signals to the student, a way for students to hold each other accountable.

The program includes short lessons on the monthly themes of empathy, self-direction, teamwork, responsibility, respect, kindness, courage, perseverance, and integrity. In addition, teachers are encouraged to begin class by being out in the hall greeting students with a positive message, to take time during class to celebrate good things that have happened, and to end the day with an inspiring message. At Marshalltown's middle school and high school, the focus has largely been on the creation of social contracts for classrooms and using them as an ongoing reference point for developing and adhering to a positive culture.

The secondary counselors' role in Marshalltown has been key to the implementation of SEL through the Positive Action guidance curriculum. Positive Action is an evidence-based program that CASEL has identified as a SELect program. It is a lesson-based approach in which counselors deliver fifteen-minute scripted lessons in classrooms or small groups, largely focused on enhancing students' positive self-concept and character development.

The program assessment conducted by the Ecological Approaches to Social Emotional Learning (EASEL) Laboratory of the Harvard Graduate School of Education found that the major emphasis of Positive Action is on identity and self-esteem and enabling students to feel good about themselves. EASEL's evaluations of the program show a reduction in at-risk behaviors.

In terms of promoting effective tier-2 and tier-3 MTSS interventions, Marshalltown provides individual and small-group mental health services, several therapeutic classrooms, and an alternative high school program that emphasizes relationship building and social-emotional development. In addition, the director of special services has developed a partnership with community mental health services. Through monthly meetings with these community partners, the district collaboratively plans and pursues strategies that not only provide intervention services for individual and small groups of students but also offer mental health education programs for parents and staff. The district also launched an SEL website for parents.

Taken together, the district has made significant inroads into implementing SEL. Central administration has led by example. In order to ensure that he had sufficient knowledge and background to make recommendations and judgments about SEL programming, Superintendent Schutte carved time out of his busy schedule in 2021–2022 to participate in an online SEL course offered by CASEL, became actively involved in AASA's SEL Cohort, and attended a three-day site visit to a district with extensive experience in implementing Responsive Classroom.

In addition to becoming a CPS trainer for the district, Matt Cretsinger was accepted into and successfully completed the CASEL Fellow program, spending the entire 2021–2022 school year delving deeply into both the nuances of SEL and its implementation. As part of his work within the district, he meets monthly with each building administrator to discuss the school's progress in moving SEL forward. These actions speak loudly to administrators and faculty about the importance of SEL and the personal investment district leaders are making to ensure its thoughtful and successful implementation.

INSIGHTS INTO IMPLEMENTATION

In Marshalltown, as elsewhere, leadership matters in the effective implementation of SEL. That the superintendent and director of special services have made a personal commitment of time to become knowledgeable about SEL and to refine their own skills demonstrates the seriousness of their individual commitment and the commitment of the district. When that investment is made by district leaders who have also made a long-term commitment to the district, the resulting stability and continuity go a long way toward moving the district forward.

It is all too easy for school administrators and faculty to try to wait out a new initiative without making substantive changes to their practice. However, when there is clear commitment to a particular direction on the part of district leaders, and when those leaders have demonstrated a long-term commitment to the district, district staff give more credence to the change and pursue it more seriously.

The change in thinking brought about by CPS strongly influenced staff openness to SEL. Listening to students, hearing their concerns, and empathizing with their struggles provided the foundation for understanding the need to support social and emotional skill development. It also helped refine the district's choice of SEL programming in that district leaders and teachers could see the value of creating caring school communities through Responsive Classroom strategies that helped children develop skills by living them and reflecting on them in the daily life of the classroom.

Professional development matters. The professional development provided to support CPS and Responsive Classroom has made a difference in people's practice, both in the classroom and in administrative offices. Admittedly, that depth has not been achieved without significant expense, but Marshalltown's intentional investment has generated a substantial and meaningful return. In providing in-depth professional development, the district's partnership with its area education agency enabled it to leverage resources that otherwise would not have been available.

While short online or in-person trainings may get things started, in the final analysis they do not produce a deep impact on practice. It is extended learning, coaching, and reflection opportunities that facilitate new teaching and administrative skills. This distinction is particularly clear when examining the implementation of CPS districtwide, as well as Responsive Classroom at the elementary level, in contrast with the execution of Capturing Kids' Hearts at the secondary level. While the very nature of elementary teachers' interactions with students has changed, secondary teachers tend to view the social contract as another way of managing the classroom rather than a way to build community.

Collaboration and partnership are effective supports to change. Marshalltown developed an important partnership with Central Rivers Area Education Agency that enabled the district to offer professional development in CPS. The district's participation in AASA's SEL Cohort and the director of special services' participation in CASEL's Fellows program gave district and school leaders the opportunity to learn from others who were implementing SEL. And the district's partnerships with local mental health agencies enabled students and families to access critical services more easily and efficiently.

CONCLUSION

As a small district with overwhelming demands on its few central office administrators, Marshalltown has made it clear that social-emotional development is essential for its overall success in supporting students' academic achievement and social-emotional well-being. In a community that has had to confront a tornado, a derecho, and a multiyear pandemic, it would have been easy to set all else aside and simply manage these crises as best they could. The district chose not to do that, but rather summoned the courage and fortitude to move forward with SEL, in part because it was a way to address students' needs resulting from these challenges and in part because it was the right thing to do for children's growth and development. In fact, in addition to pursuing its original plans, the district sought funding to enhance its efforts and succeeded in securing a multiyear state mental health grant to deepen SEL implementation.

Marshalltown Community School District acknowledges that it is still at the beginning of its work with SEL. Much more needs to be done over the coming years to extend and refine the district's SEL programming. However, the leadership has laid a solid foundation and the administrative structures are in place to move SEL forward successfully.

Chapter 6

First Steps

Moriarty–Edgewood School District (New Mexico)

Getting an initiative launched is sometimes the hardest step of implementation. For Moriarty–Edgewood School District, a rural district forty miles east of Albuquerque with limited funding and limited access to professional development opportunities, the launch of social-emotional learning has involved identifying a number of access points where faculty can feel comfortable and invested in taking modest steps forward.

Moriarty–Edgewood School District (MESD) consists of one early childhood center, three elementary schools, two middle schools, and one high school. While the district's student population is small, the territory it serves is immense. Located along the original and famed Route 66 from Chicago to Los Angeles, this high-desert district encompasses the two communities that give it its name, sprawls across the boundaries of four counties, and is roughly the size of Rhode Island. Due to the district's geographic expanse, some of its 2,300 students ride the school bus for more than an hour each way.

Over 46 percent of the students qualify as economically disadvantaged, with three of its six schools designated as Title I schools. Approximately 52 percent of the student body are Hispanic, 43 percent Caucasian, and the remainder African American, Asian, and Native American. English language learners represent 6.5 percent of the student body.

Staffing can be a challenge in rural areas; MESD has experienced difficulty in filling positions in all corners of the district, particularly during the pandemic. However, many teachers in the district have lived and worked in the region for years and a significant proportion of the administrators have risen up the ladder of responsibility within the district. That has created internal stability built upon strong interpersonal relationships.

Central administration in a district this size is thin, with only a superintendent, director of learning services, director of personnel, and director of finance, plus a special programs coordinator who covers special education and other support services. The burden of leading initiatives generally falls to the superintendent and the director of learning services. Fortunately, both of these individuals have a deep knowledge of the district and the two communities they serve.

Superintendent Teresa Salazar had been a principal in Moriarty–Edgewood before taking a position in the central office of another district. She later returned to serve for seven years as the director of learning services and has now been serving as superintendent for five years.

Natalie Romero, the director of learning services, grew up in Moriarty. She continues to live in the same community and her children attend school here. She previously served as a special education teacher, principal, and special programs coordinator. Now, as the director of learning services, she manages all areas within curriculum and instruction, as well as professional development and a wide range of miscellaneous district responsibilities. For example, for nearly two years the response to the pandemic required that she support contact tracing by making phone calls to affected families.

These two leaders' depth of knowledge about the communities they serve and about the staff and families of the district gives them a unique ability to understand the small and incremental steps that may be necessary to launch an initiative such as SEL.

PREPARING THE PATH FORWARD

The district began its SEL journey during the 2017–2018 school year, launching the training of every staff member, including bus drivers, in trauma-informed care. Realizing that many students experience adverse childhood experiences (ACEs), the district wanted to help staff understand the impact of these experiences on learning and how best to intervene.

Children impacted by trauma often cope with challenges by employing a flight, fight, freeze, or hide response, complicating communication and school participation. Understanding these responses provides teachers, administrators, and other staff with a better sense of what may be producing reactions in children when their trauma experiences have been triggered. Rather than simply viewing a child's reaction as inappropriate and unacceptable, educators familiar with trauma-informed care are more likely to understand why a child may be responding in a particular way. Trauma-informed practice can lead to educators becoming more compassionate, receptive, and responsive to students. The adults focus on paying close attention to students and on understanding each student's perspective stemming from unique—and often out-of-school—circumstances.

However, it is critical that adults avoid seeing the child only through a single-story lens of trauma. Trauma is complex, subjective, and personal, and children respond differently to traumatic events in their lives, particularly when those circumstances vary in intensity and frequency. Children's response to trauma is also influenced by the support network or lack of support surrounding them. Trauma-informed care goes beyond seeing the child as having an adjustment or coping problem to recognizing that the child also possesses agency and resilience. It recognizes that school environments may exacerbate or even generate experiences of trauma. The focus of trauma-informed care, therefore, centers not on fixing the student, but on creating environments that facilitate responsiveness and growth.

The work in applying trauma-informed care and trauma-sensitive instruction begins with providing a sense of safety, predictability, and consistency to create a productive and responsive environment. The educator's role in trauma-informed practice is to develop trusting and dependable relationships with students and provide instruction that fosters collaboration, empowerment, and cultural responsiveness (Substance Abuse and Mental Health Services Administration, 2014). These strategies are also the essence of programs that support social-emotional learning; thus, MESD's training in trauma-informed practice laid the groundwork for the district's next steps toward SEL.

Those next steps focused on extending the district's capability to respond to mental health concerns, as well as implementing a prevention effort through SEL programming. Superintendent Salazar realized that the district needed to enhance its mental health services. She advocated for the addition of four mental health professionals and received board approval for these positions.

In addition, the district implemented a virtual SEL check-in for grades K–8. This procedure allows students to report how they are feeling each day, encourages them to mention any challenges that may be upsetting them, and then sends an email to social workers if any student needs assistance.

The district began to explore classroom-based SEL efforts using the Sanford Harmony SEL curriculum in the elementary grades, giving teachers discretion to implement various elements of the program. This program was then extended to the middle school level for use during health classes. The use of Sanford Harmony evolved further in 2021–2022 with the district adopting the program's weekly lessons at the elementary and middle school levels.

At the same time, the TRAILS (Transforming Research into Action to Improve the Lives of Students) curriculum was made available to all high school students by incorporating it into required English classes. To ensure continuity with the earlier districtwide training in trauma-informed practice, the district convened a book study using *Trauma-Sensitive Leadership: Creating a Safe and Predictable School Environment* by John Eller and Tom Hierck.

In the spring of 2021, the district also joined AASA's SEL Impact Project and the AASA SEL Cohort. In taking these steps, MESD's goals were to learn from other districts, as well as to identify appropriate SEL curricula and professional development for the secondary level. As part of the SEL Impact Project, the district formed an SEL team of twelve staff members, facilitated by the director of learning services, to move SEL forward in the district. The team included mental health professionals, a principal, and elementary and middle school teachers.

To secure broader community support for SEL, the superintendent proposed an SEL goal as one of four strategic plan goals that were adopted at the board's June 2021 meeting. The goal reads "MESD will create and implement a formal system to deliver instruction and training in the area of SEL with the end goal of acquisition and application for all."

SANFORD HARMONY AND TRAILS

Sanford Harmony is an online, K–6 social-emotional learning program supported by the Inspire online professional development program. Initially developed in 2008 by a team at Arizona State University, it garnered the attention of philanthropist T. Denny Sanford, whose support enabled it to be made available without cost to all school districts wishing to use it. The program has several components including weekly lessons, everyday practices, and home-school connections.

The program provides approximately twenty weekly lessons for each grade level around five topics: diversity and inclusion, empathy and critical thinking, communications, problem-solving, and peer relations. The lessons are designed to teach social skills directly through activities and dialogue. The program also encourages teachers to use several everyday practices. These everyday practices begin with students setting goals at the beginning of the year to create the norms for the classroom. In addition, teachers are encouraged to hold a ten- to twenty-minute "meet up" each morning that involves a greeting, sharing, check-in, and quick connection activity. The meet up is similar in some ways to Responsive Classroom's morning meeting.

To encourage students to get to know each other better, one of the Sanford Harmony program components is "buddy up," in which the teacher structures the weekly pairing of students for brief buddy activities throughout the week so that by the end of the year each student has been paired with every other student in the class. The program also provides "quick connection cards" that can be used during these buddy activities, as part of the meet up time, or for integration into other classroom activities. The cards focus on such areas as community building, collaboration, and conversation. Finally, the program provides activities that parents can do at home to support the development of social skills.

Harmony has been designated as one of CASEL's SELect programs, cited for evaluation evidence that it produced greater feelings of classroom identification and school liking, fewer aggressive behaviors, and some academic gains. In another evaluation study, the Ecological

Approaches to Social Emotional Learning (EASEL) Laboratory of the Harvard Graduate School of Education found that Sanford Harmony focuses primarily on the development of prosocial and cooperation skills, as well as emotional knowledge and expression (Jones et al., 2021, p. 361).

Although some MESD teachers have used the meet-up element of Sanford Harmony, most have chosen to make more regular use of the weekly lessons, which are structured for a thirty- to forty-five-minute period on the district's early-release Wednesdays. The 2021–2022 school year marked the first time in which there was consistent use of the program across the elementary schools. Although teachers expressed support for the program, some voiced concern that there wasn't a sufficient number of lessons to stretch across the entire year.

Implementing the skill lessons without the other elements of the program was a strategic way to introduce teachers to social-emotional learning in a manner they were more comfortable with, since the lessons resembled more traditional curricula. However, without the other elements of the program, the lessons stood out more as a unit of study and less as a way to build those skills into the daily life of the classroom.

In addition, because the Inspire online professional development program is self-paced and at teachers' discretion, it does not provide the depth of support or the teacher dialogue and discussion of experiences that are necessary to give teachers a solid grounding in teaching social development and building community in their classrooms. Moriarty–Edgewood has identified these areas as focal points for the coming year.

The TRAILS (Transforming Research into Action to Improve the Lives of Students) program was developed by the University of Michigan Medical School. Its focus is on enhancing the delivery of mental health services for adolescents. TRAILS provides twenty classroom lessons aligned to the CASEL skills framework as a tier-1 support. It has not been evaluated by CASEL or EASEL. To reach all the students at the high school level in MESD, the seven teachers in the English department volunteered to incorporate the TRAILS curriculum into their classes throughout the 2021–2022 school year.

INSIGHTS INTO LAUNCHING AN SEL INITIATIVE

When a district is strapped for resources and central office staffing, finding a path to effective implementation is challenging. Even choosing which programs to adopt is a time-consuming and almost overwhelming endeavor. More than 150 curricular programs submitted applications to CASEL to be designated as SELect Programs. Many others advertise themselves to schools as providing SEL either as part of an existing curricular program or as a separate SEL program.

For a district, making clear choices that are evidence based is challenging. Finding the right professional development to support teacher capacity to implement SEL effectively is equally challenging. In such an environment, free or inexpensive online programs offer a highly attractive and reasonable place to start.

MESD's initial focus on trauma-informed practice was an effective way to begin the work. It not only introduced the staff to a student-centered approach to SEL-related practices, but also provided a rationale for going beyond mental health interventions to creating safe and supportive environments for children. Taking the next step by encouraging teachers to explore Sanford Harmony's free instructional resources and online professional development has served to foster a better understanding of the social-emotional competencies and the kinds of instructional lessons that support students' skill development.

MESD leaders also took a number of steps to solidify support for moving forward. Securing board support for SEL implementation as a strategic goal is no small achievement and served to give the community's stamp of endorsement to the district's efforts. Forming an SEL committee to broaden leadership among administrators and staff was another important step. Joining the AASA SEL Impact Project and SEL Cohort put district leaders in touch with other districts that were further along in their SEL journey and provided opportunities to learn from their experiences.

Most important, however, has been the leadership of Superintendent Salazar and Director Romero. Their commitment to and leadership of this effort and their longevity in the district have given the effort credibility and meaningfulness. Administrators and staff understand that social-emotional learning is an important initiative for moving the district and its students forward.

CONCLUSION

While Moriarty–Edgewood School District has a long way to go, it deserves credit for having laid a foundation for furthering the work in SEL. Admittedly, the district's progress was unavoidably slowed by the many impacts of the COVID pandemic. Not only did staff and student absences interrupt planned activities, the lean administrative staff had no choice but to relegate some of their preferred activities to a back burner as such added responsibilities as daily contact tracing consumed their workday.

Beginning in 2021–2022, district leaders resumed looking ahead with much eagerness to the difference that SEL could make in their student outcomes. In particular, investing in a deeper level of professional development in 2022–2023 will be a significant boost to the effectiveness of SEL in the classroom. The steps that MESD leaders have taken have opened the door. The challenge they now face is taking the staff to a higher level of understanding of SEL and to more integrated and cohesive approaches to its implementation.

Given their limited resources, it is likely that MESD's journey will continue to be one of small, incremental steps. However, the low level of staff turnover will be in their favor as teachers and administrators have an opportunity to expand their skills and deepen their professional practice over time. The strength of their commitment to a common goal will be a critical factor in enhancing the extent of their success.

Chapter 7

Targeting SEL Standards

Naperville Community Unit School District 203 (Illinois)

While most districts select evidence-based SEL programs with a reputation for success and customize them to align with the culture and instructional program of the district, Naperville Community Unit School District 203 chose a different path. Viewing the development of social and emotional skills to be as essential as the development of any area of academic competency, the district decided to integrate SEL deeply and seamlessly into the fabric of daily instruction by building on a set of SEL standards.

As a standards-based district in academics, Naperville 203 focused on teaching to SEL standards, assessing progress along those standards, and, at the elementary level, even reporting that progress on a standards-based report card. Both academic and social-emotional learning targets are designed into teachers' lessons, posted in the classroom, and reviewed with the class so that students understand the meaning and value of what they are learning.

The process followed a trajectory of alignment, professional development, and implementation—similar to the adoption of academic curricula. Although it took years to reach this point, the district has been successful in integrating SEL into daily instruction and classroom culture.

Naperville 203's success derives from both its administrative leadership and its financial capacity to support a thorough process of curriculum development and alignment. Naperville is an affluent suburban district forty miles west of Chicago. The school district serves almost seventeen thousand pre-K through grade 12 students in two high schools, five junior highs, fourteen elementary schools, and one early childhood center. Approximately 61 percent of the students are white; 18 percent are Asian; 11 percent are Hispanic/Latino; 5 percent are Black; and 5 percent are American Indian, Native Hawaiian, or multiracial. English learners make up 7 percent of the student population, low-income students represent 16 percent, and the proportion of homeless students is under 1 percent. With per-pupil spending that is well above the state average, it is one of the highest-performing school districts in the state of Illinois.

EVOLUTION OF SEL PROGRAMMING IN NAPERVILLE 203

Dan Bridges, Naperville 203's superintendent, joined the district in 2011 as assistant superintendent for secondary education and was appointed to the superintendent position the following year. As one of his early actions, he proposed the development of a five-year strategic blueprint. During the 2013–2014 school year, the district launched an intensive strategic planning and community engagement process that included faculty, administration, parents, and community members.

The resulting blueprint, Focus 2020, launched the strategic SEL initiative in Naperville. One of the strategies to reach the district's goal of "designing and implementing effective practices that promote learning for all," was, by the target date of June 30, 2018, to "develop and implement an effective social emotional plan that will enable students to demonstrate the skills needed to be competent in their families, with their peers, in their school, at their work settings, and in their communities."

To get the SEL initiative off the ground, the district formed a staff steering committee led by the assistant superintendent for student services and the director of student services. The committee began by working with CASEL to develop a vision, mission, and set of core beliefs. Their vision statement articulated where they wanted to be in the future—that "all students will utilize social, emotional and academic skills in order to become resourceful and resilient life-long learners."

Based on this vision, they set the mission of SEL integration as "we cultivate resourceful, resilient citizens by teaching social, emotional and academic skills in a nurturing learning environment." In order to provide a framework for developing and implementing SEL curricula, the steering committee articulated a set of belief statements that established the foundation for the direction the district would take:

- All students need a balance of academic and social-emotional learning.
- Students learn and apply SEL skills when they are explicitly and intentionally integrated into daily lessons.
- A positive school culture and climate is the foundation for all social and emotional learning.
- All stakeholders are responsible for contributing to the ongoing development of SEL skills.

The steering committee also identified four mutually supportive strategies to achieve this vision and mission. These strategies included developing the expertise of staff; creating a comprehensive, district-wide curriculum; fostering a positive climate and culture in schools; and building parent partnerships. The district launched work in each of these strategies in 2015–2016 and placed Lisa Xagas, then director of student services and a champion of SEL, in charge of leading these efforts. As one of its first action steps, the administration formed a curriculum team to create SEL curriculum maps for each grade from early childhood through grade 12. Another committee was formed to establish parent and community partnerships.

An intensive professional development program was launched to build the capacity of two to four teacher leaders from each school, who would not only learn about SEL, but would also open their classrooms to other teachers to observe SEL in action and would lead professional development sessions for their faculty. To build the expertise of staff, the district developed a series of nine learning modules that were delivered by the SEL teacher leaders in their schools across three school years (2015–2016 through 2017–2018) focusing on the what and why of SEL, adult SEL competencies, and implementation of the SEL curriculum.

The learning modules shared the SEL vision, mission, and beliefs with the entire faculty, making it clear that teachers needed to explicitly teach and intentionally integrate SEL skills into academic content. The modules focused on how teachers could provide direct instruction in social-emotional skills through building social and emotional learning targets into core instruction. For example, a guided reading lesson might also include learning targets around active listening and taking turns. In addition, the modules provided teachers with resources to help them create positive learning environments in classrooms that modeled social and emotional skills through such strategies as morning meetings and class meetings.

The process of curriculum development and mapping built on the Illinois Social Emotional Learning Standards. It took eighteen months of work by the SEL curriculum committee to develop curriculum maps and content recommendations. The implementation of the SEL curriculum coincided with the last year of professional development in 2017–2018 and set an expectation that every teacher's lessons would include both academic and social-emotional learning targets. At that point, believing that "it was imperative that our assessments measure skill attainment similarly to core content areas such as literacy or math" (Igoe and Xagas, 2018), the district began to develop and pilot its own SEL assessment rubrics and standards-based reporting tools.

Building on this foundation, the district continued to extend the integration of SEL into basic district processes. The district developed "look-fors" for administrators and learning support coaches to use when they worked with teachers on their professional growth and performed classroom observations. SEL was included in the district's new educator program for new employees. SEL was also built into the school improvement process.

Building principals were responsible for developing an SEL school improvement goal and a school-based action plan in support of that goal. Building principals and their SEL teacher leaders were also expected to gather and provide evidence of implementation in their school improvement plan reports.

School counselors and social workers delivered SEL programs in classrooms as well. SEL was integrated into the multi-tiered system of supports (MTSS) process, using SEL curricula such as Second Step and Habits of Mind for tier-1 and tier-2 interventions to address lagging skills in social and emotional areas. The district provided district-wide training in de-escalation strategies and trauma-informed practices to support MTSS and SEL. The district's equity initiative built on and aligned with its SEL efforts. All of these efforts enhanced the depth of implementation across the district.

Implementing SEL at the high school level is challenging for all districts. Although Naperville's high school teachers had developed SEL learning targets for their classrooms, the administration believed more could be done.

Beginning in January 2022, the high schools restructured their schedules to include two 45-minute advisory periods with staff assigned to follow a group of students throughout their high school journey. The periods are used not only to check in with students but to offer additional time for SEL curricula, academic intervention, and tiered SEL supports. In its first semester of implementation, the advisory period followed a monthly thematic approach with each month addressing one of the five CASEL social-emotional competencies. The refinement of approaches to SEL at the high school level is an ongoing goal for the years ahead.

While pleased with its accomplishments thus far in districtwide implementation of SEL, the district continues to learn from its experience and to find areas that need further development. The pandemic made it abundantly clear that adults, too, require social-emotional care and thoughtfulness beyond learning how to nurture social-emotional skills in the classroom. The stress and exhaustion brought on by teaching during the pandemic served to focus the district's efforts on creating uplifting opportunities for staff and ensuring that staff knew they were valued and appreciated.

Administrators read positive psychology literature such as *The Power of Moments* (Heath and Heath, 2017) and *The Orange Frog* (Achor, 2012) to glean ideas for investing positive energy and caring support in their staff, and they focused on creating caring communities for staff just as they had for children. To support staff, administration rolled out a "Be the Spark" initiative to encourage positivity by expressing gratitude to others through handwritten notes, compliment slamming, and fun activities within the school and at meetings.

The continuing surge in the pandemic during the 2021–2022 school year exacerbated the stress and exhaustion of staff and caused the district to work more personally and deeply on staff concerns, delaying some of the positive psychology initiatives. However, adult SEL remains a major goal for future years.

At the same time, with a growing diversity of students in the district and a concern about achievement and opportunity gaps among racial and ethnic groups, the district invested in a significant equity initiative with an emphasis on cultural proficiency and responsive school cultures. In addition, based on the lessons learned from its SEL curriculum implementation, the district is launching a revision process labeled "SEL 2.0" that will not only update the curriculum maps but will address issues of equity within the SEL framework and build on the revised CASEL framework that incorporates equity. To pursue this work, the district is reestablishing its SEL steering committee.

The district does not see its work on SEL, MTSS, and equity as separate initiatives. District leadership continues to frame all of these efforts under an umbrella of developing inclusive school communities that ensure the success of all children.

A STANDARDS-BASED APPROACH

As the first state to publish social and emotional learning standards, Illinois worked closely with CASEL to develop a curriculum framework for SEL. Illinois's SEL standards serve to achieve three overarching goals (see textbox 7.1).

Using the Illinois state standards and benchmarks for social and emotional learning, Naperville developed a detailed scope and sequence for teaching social-emotional competencies and made it accessible online for all staff.

In addition to establishing goals and learning standards, the state delineated benchmarks and performance descriptors for each of the standards for grades 1 through 8 and for grades 9 and 10 and grades 11 and 12. The district's EC–12 curriculum committee used this information to provide teachers with an online grade-by-grade curriculum map outlining the logical progression of skill development across the years. Each map includes a list of the yearlong SEL benchmarks, links to instructional strategies, vocabulary to be mastered by the end of the year, and benchmark rubrics to chart progress.

The maps provide suggested resources for launching SEL in the first weeks of school in the three broad areas of building a positive

7.1 Implementing Social-Emotional Learning

ILLINOIS SOCIAL EMOTIONAL LEARNING STANDARDS

Goal 1: Develop self-awareness and self-management skills to achieve school and life success.
    Learning Standard A: Identify and manage one's emotions and behavior.
    Learning Standard B: Recognize personal qualities and external supports.
    Learning Standard C: Demonstrate skills related to achieving personal and academic goals.

Goal 2: Use social-awareness and interpersonal skills to establish and maintain positive relationships.
    Learning Standard A: Recognize the feelings and perspectives of others.
    Learning Standard B: Recognize individual and group similarities and differences.
    Learning Standard C: Use communication and social skills to interact effectively with others.
    Learning Standard D: Demonstrate an ability to prevent, manage, and resolve interpersonal conflicts in constructive ways.

Goal 3: Demonstrate decision-making skills and responsible behaviors in personal, school, and community contexts.
    Learning Standard A: Consider ethical, safety, and societal factors in making decisions.
    Learning Standard B: Apply decision-making skills to deal responsibly with daily academic and social situations.
    Learning Standard C: Contribute to the well-being of one's school and community.

(Illinois State Board of Education, 2022)

classroom culture, establishing expectations for learning behaviors, and building a culture of collaboration. The curriculum maps also list resources for teaching each of the competencies and benchmarks, along with suggestions for explicit instruction as well as integration opportunities. Finally, the maps suggest observable behaviors that illustrate the performance descriptors in the state standards that students should be able to demonstrate once they achieve the goal.

Depending on grade level, the suggested resources are often drawn from such programs as Second Step, Activities for Building Character and Social-Emotional Learning, and Developing Habits of Mind. Program materials and books were provided to all elementary teachers. At the secondary level, the district provides suggestions for strategies that align with each goal, cross-referencing them to state or national standards in the chosen curricular area.

Critical to the effective implementation of SEL has been the expectation that every instructional lesson will have both an academic and a social-emotional learning target and that they will be explicitly displayed in the classroom. For example, in a first-grade classroom, a teacher had posted the SEL learning target as "What does it mean to be a good friend?" In one fifth-grade classroom, the SEL learning target was framed as an "I can" statement: "I can listen to others with empathy and understanding." In another fifth-grade classroom the learning target was "I can set a goal and make an action plan toward progress." In an elementary learning commons, which is an updated version of a media center with integrated maker spaces, the Learning Center teacher had posted two targets: "I am a responsible digital citizen" and "I can show I am ready to learn."

Building this expectation of displayed targets into the teacher observation and evaluation process has given the requirement force and has led to much greater consistency and focus in classroom instruction.

PROFESSIONAL DEVELOPMENT

Many commercial SEL programs provide their own scope and sequence with well-delineated instructional lessons and activities. Naperville's approach of focusing on standards and benchmarks along with recommended resources, rather than a program, gives teachers greater discretion but correspondingly increases their responsibility and workload. To provide support for this model, the district provides extensive professional development and utilizes school-based teacher leaders and teachers' professional learning communities (PLCs) to foster more consistency in approach and integration into daily instruction.

Developing school-based teacher leaders in a train-the-trainer model was critical to consistent implementation. Initiated in 2015–2016, two to four teachers at each school were selected to receive stipends for their appointment as SEL teacher leaders. The responsibilities were extensive. Each teacher leader participated in fifteen hours of training to enhance their understanding of SEL and SEL best practices. Bringing those practices into their daily instruction, they opened their classrooms for other teachers to observe SEL in action. They also collaborated with building leadership to plan and facilitate building-based professional development.

To support these teacher leaders, the district provided in-person and online opportunities for them to share experiences and engage in coaching discussions. In addition, the district developed the nine professional learning modules discussed earlier for teacher leaders to use with their faculties across three years.

The first year of professional development for faculties at the schools focused on building a foundation of understanding of SEL, the rationale for giving it significant attention, and what effective SEL practice looks like in the classroom. For example, developing positive learning environments includes such strategies as morning meetings that serve to promote a sense of care and community in elementary classrooms.

The second year focused on preparing to launch SEL practices, concentrating on the classroom strategies and resources. The third year focused on implementing SEL with fidelity. The teacher leaders have continued to open their classrooms for observation, provide coaching for teachers, and facilitate PLCs and professional development sessions focused on SEL. Also, because of the expectation for posting social-emotional learning targets and the inclusion of social-emotional benchmarks on the elementary report card, the teacher leaders are seen as valuable resources for enabling teachers to meet those expectations.

Professional development has continued beyond the initial years of training. SEL professional development was built into training for all new teachers and administrators. In addition, since some students who receive tier-2 or tier-3 services in a special setting may still need extra tier-1 support while in their regular classrooms, the district provided all teachers with extensive training in de-escalation strategies and trauma-informed practices. These trainings became even more critical due to the trauma some students experienced throughout the pandemic and the lag in social skills that many experienced as a result of online and hybrid learning.

The district has also provided initial professional development for administrators in restorative justice practices, although the work in this area was interrupted by the pandemic. For 2022–2023, the district created the position of director of outreach and student belonging and filled it with two individuals who will focus across all grade levels on both SEL and restorative practices. In addition, each high school has been able to hire two student advocacy specialists who staff a community resource center, which is an alternative to suspension. They are trained in how to implement restorative practices at the high school level.

ASSESSING PROGRESS

In a standards-based model, it is vitally important to be able not only to assess whether students are developing the skills to meet the standards but also to determine whether the curriculum and its implementation are effective. Because the committee that was convened to review and develop assessments did not find anything that aligned well with Illinois state standards or the district's philosophy, the members decided to develop their own formative instrument by incorporating performance-based rubrics to assess student progress in meeting the standards. They chose to apply the first three reporting standards that are used for measuring progress on academic standards: beginning, approaching, and secure. They chose not to use exemplary, which is used in measuring academic progress.

Because of the explicit district focus on the development of social and emotional skills, the curriculum committee decided these skills should be reported on students' standards-based progress reports so that parents could be aware of their children's progress in this area. For example, the fourth-grade student progress report includes the following SEL standards:

- Describes ways to express emotions in a socially acceptable manner
- Sets a short-term goal and monitors progress toward achieving the goal
- Identifies situational cues that indicate how others may feel
- Demonstrates how to work effectively with others
- Identifies and applies the steps of systemic decision making

To support elementary teachers in reporting on these standards, the curriculum committee developed a guidebook that includes the standard, the performance rubric, and potential areas of evidence to document progress. A similar set of standards for middle school has been piloted in two of the district's middle schools. Broader implementation at the middle school level will take place in 2023–2024. Implementing this addition to the progress report entailed extensive professional development for faculty within their PLCs.

Reporting on social-emotional development on the student progress report not only stimulates interest in the development of these skills at home but also leads to greater collaboration between teachers and parents in supporting student progress. It also helps refine the district's curricular approach. For example, aggregating the information on student progress reports revealed a general lag in skill acquisition in fourth-grade students in the area of establishing and monitoring their progress toward goals. The district was then able to add additional resources and instructional tools to the curriculum maps to enable teachers to better address that area of skill development.

The district also uses other measures to confirm that its SEL efforts are making a difference. After the first year of implementation, the chronic absenteeism rate declined as did the number of mental health hospitalizations. These indicators continued to show positive results in the following years, despite the impact of the pandemic.

The district also surveyed all teachers about their perceptions of the effects of SEL implementation. Over 90 percent of elementary teachers reported that the SEL curriculum had a positive impact on individual students and on their classrooms' climate. Reflecting the greater challenges of implementation at the secondary level, fewer middle and high school teachers (but still more than 70 percent) reported that the SEL curriculum had a positive impact on their students and classrooms.

PARENT ENGAGEMENT

To help parents understand the addition to the student progress report and to encourage parents to partner in the work of social-emotional development, the district created grade-level "SEL Snapshots." These one-page resources for parents list the typical social and emotional skills, vocabulary, and priority benchmarks that are the focus of that grade. Each one-pager includes some "home connections" of ways for parents to help their child develop these skills, along with links and resources parents can tap to learn more. The resource pages also include indicators of whether a child may need extra support in particular areas, such as if the child is exhibiting a loss of interest, changes in sleep habits, or periods of sadness.

The SEL Snapshots are available on the district website for all parents. They are distributed at school open houses and curriculum nights. They are also used by teachers in their meetings with parents.

EQUITY

The district views SEL as an essential element in its effort to ensure equity for all students and has made it integral to its 2020–2023 equity plan. Formally launching its equity initiative in 2019, the district brought on board executive director of diversity and inclusion Dr. Rakeda Leaks to lead the ongoing work in this area. Reflecting on the persistent racial, ethnic, and economic-related disparities in academic performance and school experience, the district set forth a bold diversity and inclusion belief statement:

> Naperville Community Unit School District 203 appreciates, affirms, and is inclusive of the range of differences in people and ideas. Cultivating a culture of inclusion exemplifies our belief that an exemplary school district, *"values the dignity and uniqueness of each individual."* We are committed to creating an environment where diversity and inclusion is evident in who we are and what we do. We seek to identify and address inequities and all forms of discrimination and intolerance. We believe it is the responsibility of our school district to offer students a diverse set of experiences and perspectives that will better prepare them to thrive in an inclusive, global community and world. (Naperville 203 Community Unit School District, n.d.a)

The district followed up with a comprehensive equity plan targeted at fulfilling this commitment. The district also formed a diversity advisory committee to provide feedback and direction. The committee includes two representatives of each school, one of whom is a parent or caregiver, as well as representatives from the central office and board. The equity efforts are deeply tied to and coordinated with other district initiatives. As articulated in the equity plan document, "[t]he Plan also works in tandem with other district-wide efforts such as the Multi-tiered Systems of Support (MTSS) and Social-Emotional Learning (SEL) plans in a coordinated system to ensure that every student thrives and achieves at their fullest potential" (Naperville 203 Community School Unit, n.d.b, p. 8).

Creating equity-centered classrooms is one of five pillars of success in the equity plan. As Jayne Willard, assistant superintendent for curriculum and instruction, writes in explaining the meaning of equity-centered classrooms, "Equity-centered classrooms begin with inclusive environments that promote respectful and authentic relationships between teachers and students and among students. Our SEL curriculum sets the foundation for creating a positive school culture and classroom environment" (Naperville 203 Community School Unit, n.d.c).

The equity plan involved extensive professional development on faculty professional days with themes such as tone and trust, personal culture and personal journey, from social dominance to social justice, and classroom and job-specific implications and applications. The initiative also involved the formation of building-based equity teams. The connection and coordination among the SEL, MTSS, and equity initiatives enhance each of these efforts and offer greater clarity to the administrators and teachers who are implementing them.

INSIGHTS INTO IMPLEMENTATION

Naperville's ten-year history in the development and implementation of SEL offers numerous insights into which strategies have been instrumental in the district's success. First among these is the importance of administrative leadership, particularly on the part of the superintendent. Dan Bridges not only believes in the critical nature of SEL for student success but repeatedly articulates that belief to staff, parents, and the community. His eleven-year tenure has provided consistency, continuity, and stability and he has remained steadfast throughout those years in his support for SEL.

Superintendent Bridges has also designated central office leadership for the SEL plan to highlight its importance and ensure it is effectively pursued. Lisa Xagas, now assistant superintendent for student services, has served as a leader and champion of SEL across much of that period, providing valuable insight and support for the deep integration of SEL into district curricula, instruction, professional development, and administrative processes.

In addition to leadership, the broad-based strategic planning process that resulted in SEL becoming one of the district's priority actions ensured commitment on the part of the board, staff, and parents. By having a plan that emerged from the community, SEL's importance was not simply the agenda of one person but part of a districtwide effort to educate the whole child. Dan Bridges and his leadership team were seen as carrying forward the community's hopes, aspirations, and commitments.

Although it is challenging for less well-funded districts to tackle the kind of methodical curriculum mapping and development process that Naperville pursued, key aspects of its approach are replicable. The commitment to build slowly and carefully—and to provide carefully thought-through documents outlining goals, standards, benchmarks, instructional strategies, and resources—clearly assisted in the initiative's translation to classroom and school.

The district has continued to request feedback from teachers and refine the curriculum along the way, thereby providing greater acceptance and effectiveness. That the development of an SEL curriculum followed the same path as any academic area spoke volumes about the seriousness with which administrators and teachers viewed this effort.

Clearly, one area that dramatically stands out as boosting Naperville's implementation efforts is the requirement for every lesson to have both an academic learning target and an SEL learning target and to have these targets specifically articulated in the lesson plan and displayed in the classroom. That one requirement brings SEL into the daily instructional program of every classroom in the district.

When that explicit requirement is also part of the teacher growth and evaluation process, teacher observations, student progress reports, and MTSS intervention processes, it builds a wrap-around sense of its intimate integration into all aspects of instruction. The pervasive embedding of SEL into such a wide range of instructional and management systems not only makes a statement about its importance; it demonstrates that SEL is not a separate curriculum but an overarching element of effective teaching and learning.

The strategy of identifying two to four teacher leaders in each school and affirming the importance of their efforts through stipends to serve as classroom models, professional development facilitators, and coaches proved to be exceptionally effective. Teachers are more likely to listen to other teachers and learn from each other. This strategy encourages teacher leaders to develop deep expertise in SEL and to continue to refine their own classroom SEL instruction.

The teacher leaders' ability to assist other teachers in their school provides just-in-time support for teachers seeking help. In addition, the district was thoughtful about providing these teacher leaders with professional development modules and ongoing PLC support so that there was a greater level of districtwide consistency in the transmission of concepts and strategies.

The district undertook three large areas of work over the past several years in expanding its MTSS, SEL, and equity efforts. Rather than treating these initiatives as separate tracks, uniting them under the theme of building inclusive school communities has brought all three efforts together in a cohesive and mutually supportive way. By having the work framed in this manner, staff can be clear about the overall vision and see how each facet supports the vision. In fact, each of these areas relies on the others to be most effective. That understanding is an important insight, not only for district staff but for the field in general.

The focus on positive psychology to support adult SEL and enhance the sense of community and resilience among adults came later in the initiative but at a critical point in the recovery from the pandemic. Although this effort is still a developing aspect of the district's SEL work, the exploration of strategies can offer further insights into how best to support faculty as well as students. One of the important insights articulated by district administration is that a focus on adult

SEL earlier in the initiative would have been a way of providing better support to staff as well as modeling SEL strategies for them.

CONCLUSION

Naperville's long-term efforts to effectively implement SEL have reached into almost every aspect of district operations in ways that are well designed and comprehensive. Treating SEL as equivalent to any academic area and taking a methodical, comprehensive, plan-based approach to its development and dissemination have produced a highly successful model.

Districts with fewer internal resources may find it challenging to follow Naperville's path. However, the very fact that a high-performing, well-resourced district has given SEL such a significant priority can be encouraging for other districts. The manner in which Naperville views SEL as critical to students' academic and life success and is willing to take the time to deeply embed it in instructional practice serves as a beacon for others. Naperville's model is valid and effective across all grade levels and subject areas; even smaller and less financially advantaged districts will find within it adaptable elements that could serve as guides for their own SEL journey.

Chapter 8

Making SEL Foundational
Corvallis School District (Oregon)

For the leadership of the Corvallis School District, SEL is more than an additional program to be integrated into the school day. It's the foundation for the way people treat each other, it's the way classrooms are organized, and it's an essential element in delivering effective instruction. Superintendent Ryan Noss, who has led the district since 2016, believes that SEL humanizes education by building connectedness, supporting understanding, and fostering social, emotional, and cognitive development.

Superintendent Noss views the public schools as one of the few places where everyone in a community comes together. Therefore, it's the school's place to help children engage with those who come from different backgrounds, and it is the school's responsibility to give children the opportunity to practice building bridges that span differences.

He also believes that SEL is the lever to support equity and the health and wellness of children—two of the six major goals approved by the Corvallis School Board in its five-year strategic plan launched in 2018. The district articulated its vision as "We are committed to equitable access to an inclusive and rigorous learning experience and outcome that honors each student's race, culture, socioeconomic status, language, ability, gender, gender expression, and sexual orientation, resulting in engaged citizens and leaders of the future" (Corvallis School District, 2022, p. 2).

That vision statement and the district's goals are deeply embedded in the improvement goals for each of Corvallis's schools. Pursuing them, however, has been a complex process, exacerbated by the challenges of coping with the pandemic for several years. As a result, SEL programming has deeper roots at the elementary level than at the secondary.

At the elementary level, the district adopted curricula in both reading and math that facilitate the development of social skills as part of instruction. In addition, the district adopted the Center for the Collaborative Classroom's Caring School Community (CSC) social development program. CSC is a second-generation refinement of its highly effective predecessor, the Child Development Project.

CSC focuses on creating responsive and inclusive classroom communities through daily morning circles and closing meetings, regular class meetings, a cross-age buddies program, schoolwide community-building activities, family connection activities, and a positive and developmental approach to discipline. Weaving together a focus on creating caring classroom communities with curriculum and instruction that integrate social and emotional development, SEL has become the major thread throughout the school day. It also provides staff with a coherent vision, a cohesive instructional program, and the permission and support to form deeper connections with the children in their classrooms and schools and with each other.

At the secondary level, the district has focused on CharacterStrong as its middle school SEL program and Sources of Strength at the high school. The work here has begun more recently, and district leadership is seeking ways to expand or build upon these initiatives.

A DIVERSE UNIVERSITY COMMUNITY

Corvallis is home to Oregon State University; however, it is more than simply a university town. Instead, much like other communities along the I-5 corridor through the Willamette Valley, Corvallis is characterized by a high level of diversity and a significant number of families living in poverty. Among the more than 6,300 members of the student body, 32 percent qualify for free or reduced-price lunch. Fifty-seven languages are spoken in the homes of Corvallis's students and 14 percent of the students are English language learners. Demographically, the student population is 66 percent White, 18 percent Hispanic, 9 percent multiracial, and 5 percent Asian.

Oregon, although generally a progressive state in terms of education, has faced significant financial constraints that have compromised the ability of school districts to provide the kind and quality of services that are present in many other states. Based on data collected by *U.S. News and World Report*, in 2022 Oregon ranks 42nd in high school graduation rate and 37th in funding for public education. The latter figure is up significantly from earlier years due to the passage of new state funding streams.

Corvallis has seven elementary schools, two of which are dual-language schools, plus a K–8 school, and a K–5 charter school. At the secondary level, the district has two middle schools for grades 6–8 (in addition to the middle grades at the K–8 school), two high schools, and a number of transition and support programs.

State report cards for districts and schools focus on reading and math scores for all students as well as subgroups. The district has been clear that its investment in SEL and content curricula that provide consistent support for social and emotional development is the right way to enhance students' cognitive growth and academic progress. That commitment is bolstered by an administrative structure that has vested SEL leadership responsibility in curriculum and instruction leaders for each level—elementary, middle, and high.

THE EVOLUTION OF SEL IN CORVALLIS: ELEMENTARY PROGRAMS

The evolution of Corvallis's SEL efforts was not the result of a strategic SEL plan but rather an organic unfolding from one initiative to the next as administrators and teachers felt the need and saw the opportunity for that next step. As with Marshalltown (see chapter 5), the journey began as the district engaged in professional development around the Collaborative Problem Solving (CPS) program developed by Stuart Ablon and Ross Green.

The underlying principles of CPS are (1) that kids will do well if they can, and (2) that adults need to listen to children with compassion in order to identify the lagging skills that need further development as well as the classroom and instructional barriers that are getting in students' way of that development.

CPS helped shift the mindset of both administrators and teachers in Corvallis. In initially pursuing CPS, Superintendent Noss was seeking to move away from the external rewards system of Positive Behavioral

Interventions and Support (PBIS) to a greater focus on care and understanding and a belief in the goodness of kids. He framed that work as humanizing the culture of school and the relationships adults have with children. The classroom needs to become an "aspirational community," in which individuals have empathy for each other and support each other in their growth and development.

The first opportunity to embody that ethos in curriculum and instruction came through the district's adoption of a new elementary literacy program. In 2017–2018, led by Corvallis's elementary program coordinator Amy Lesan, the district undertook a relatively traditional approach to program adoption. They formed a review committee of teachers and administrators as an adoption group, developed criteria to compare programs, identified literacy curricula to review, set up a process for piloting multiple programs, and targeted board approval for the spring.

Given the weight that the district's goals placed on equity and the belief that student identity neither predicts nor predetermines success in school, the rubric to assess each literacy program included diversity within the program's literature, with an expectation that all students could see themselves in the materials. The rubric also included instructional processes that facilitated all students' full engagement and participation in instruction.

Accordingly, the English Language Arts Adoption Group that was convened to make a program recommendation was not only looking for alignment with the key elements of reading in the Common Core Standards, but also alignment with the principles embodied in universal design for learning (UDL) and culturally relevant teaching (CRT).

The adoption group initially reviewed more than ten literacy programs, narrowing the list down to two programs for the pilot phase. One was a commercial program from a major publisher and was included on the state textbook adoption list. The other was a program titled Collaborative Literacy, delivered by a nonprofit called the Center for the Collaborative Classroom (CCC).

Collaborative Literacy was not on the state list, meaning that the district would have to defend its adoption to the Oregon Department of Education. However, the program's approach to teaching reading, the diversity of literature it used, and the collaborative learning processes embedded in instruction resonated with the adoption group's teachers and administrators.

That resonance soon extended to the pilot teachers, who noted that not only was their literacy instruction helping children learn to read, but the instructional processes within the curriculum were facilitating children's social skill development. What also stood out to the pilot teachers and adoption group was the contrast in the quality of professional development provided by the two finalist programs.

While the commercial program provided an introductory workshop that struck teachers as akin to marketing, including gift cards to a local restaurant and brewery, the teachers attending the Collaborative Classroom's introductory workshops sensed that they were learning new strategies for teaching reading, writing, and comprehension as well as how to build a reading community in their classroom. There was virtually unanimous support among the pilot teachers and the adoption group for recommending Collaborative Literacy to the school board for approval. In May 2018, the board voted to approve its adoption.

One of the strong supports offered by Collaborative Literacy is an in-depth and continuing professional development program. CCC not only provides highly trained reading specialists to lead their professional development, but also identifies a liaison who serves as a critical connection with the district over time.

The liaison to Corvallis, Veronica Vasquez, had been a teacher, instructional coach, principal, and curriculum and instruction director prior to joining CCC. In her role supporting Corvallis's implementation, she has modeled lessons in classrooms and led learning walks, professional development sessions, and grade-level dialogues. She has worked with each elementary principal to formulate an individual school implementation plan. She believes that professional learning has to be job-embedded. She is clear that you can't give people a binder and hope they look at it; you need to facilitate in-depth understanding and ownership.

Through Amy Lesan's leadership, the district has provided extensive professional learning opportunities to support implementation. Teachers are organized into professional learning communities (PLCs) that meet during their one-hour early release every Friday as well as during their monthly two-hour early release. These PLCs have consistently focused on curriculum implementation of Collaborative Literacy as well as CCC's social development program Caring School Community, including Zoom calls with the CCC liaison.

To provide even greater professional learning support in the future, the CCC liaison and district leadership are training two teachers at each elementary school, one at the primary level and one at the upper grades, to be teacher leaders who can offer demonstration lessons and facilitate learning walks and professional development sessions for new teachers.

The depth of commitment among district leadership is continually demonstrated by the fact that the superintendent, the elementary curriculum coordinator, and all elementary principals attend the professional development sessions and participate in classroom learning walks—not only to support implementation but to continue learning how they can be more effective as instructional leaders.

By 2022–2023, with Corvallis in its fifth year of implementation, CCC's liaison continued to provide learning walks for principals and ongoing professional development for faculty in which the superintendent participated. This continuity and depth of professional development is a unique feature that has led to much greater fidelity of implementation as well as confidence among teachers implementing the program.

In their first year of implementing Collaborative Literacy, Corvallis's teachers discovered that CCC also provides a program—Caring School Community—that focuses on building caring classroom communities and fostering children's social development. Teachers found that the communication and collaboration strategies embedded in the literacy program's instructional practices were particularly effective at engaging students in learning. They believed that Caring School Community would enhance that engagement and brought the program to the attention of administration as a potential second element of the elementary curricular change.

Many teachers were already informally using elements such as morning circles or class meetings. They felt the structure provided by Caring School Community, as well as the sense of community it engendered among students, would address some of the behavioral issues they were confronting and make learning both more enjoyable and effective for children.

Much like Collaborative Literacy, Caring School Community came with well-planned and in-depth professional development for teachers, instructional assistants, and other staff. Although not formally adopted by the board, incorporation of the program was supported by both administration and the board and implementation began in 2019.

As with other instruction, the two years of the pandemic presented significant challenges to implementing these programs. However, program structures such as morning circles, closing meetings, and class meetings became the glue that held classes together across the virtual learning environment. As the pandemic dragged on, instructional practices became more fragmented and eventually required a targeted refocus on consistent implementation when students returned to in-class instruction in the fall of 2021.

The third interlocking piece of the elementary curriculum puzzle entailed the search for a new math program. Teachers and administrators focused their quest on identifying a math program that engages students through inquiry and investigation and embeds collaborative processes within the instruction.

As a result of this informed search, the district adopted the Bridges in Mathematics curriculum developed by an Oregon-based nonprofit, the Math Learning Center. This program is inquiry oriented and focuses on helping students develop conceptual understanding of math along with skill in applying mathematical procedures and algorithms. Students engage in collaborative problem-solving using manipulatives, visual models, games, and apps. Students propose a variety of strategies for reaching an answer and develop multiple mathematical thinking strategies through their discussion. The program uses collaborative problem-solving and student dialogue as critical elements for deepening mathematical understanding.

Underlying all of these programs is a student-centered and asset-based approach to learning and a focus on collaboration and relationships as ways to build a strong learning community. This shift in mindset about teaching and learning has had a profound impact on other aspects of school life. It has enhanced the inclusiveness of classroom environments, particularly for students with disabilities, who are now more regularly and effectively included in classroom instruction. It also has spurred interest among teachers and administrators in UDL strategies that further promote inclusiveness by affirming the diversity in students' learning strategies. Teachers have grown to understand that success doesn't need to mean the same thing for every student or be demonstrated in the same way.

The shift in mindset has deeply influenced the operation of student support teams and changed the nature of the conversations in those meetings. The meetings begin with what is appreciated about the student and what positive student traits the adults may have overlooked. Rather than considering misbehavior in terms of control, consequences, and remediation, the team attempts to see the behavior through the student's perspective and to understand what purposes the behavior may be serving for the child, which skills may be lagging, and how best to support that student's development. As one principal said, "Our job is to provide dignity for vulnerable children so that every child knows they are seen and appreciated."

This new mindset has also impacted discipline. Framing discipline issues as mistakes to learn from through repair of relationships, restitution of property, and other restorative strategies is a significant change for teachers and students. It replaces methods that tend to push out marginalized groups of students with approaches that focus on bringing students back into the community with dignity. Rather than teachers calling students out for their behavior, they are calling students in and slowing down to listen to children's perspective.

The understanding among staff is that everyone has skills they are working on, everyone makes mistakes, and everyone is doing the best they can with the skills they have. The school's role is to understand where the student is and help them develop skills in lagging areas by helping them constructively learn from their mistakes.

The collaborative strategies embodied in Bridges in Mathematics, Collaborative Literacy, and Caring School Community provide continuity across the day for students. Each element builds upon the others to create positive learning environments that nurture students' social skills. Principals report they are seeing not only improved academic performance but also improved collaboration skills, management of emotions, ability to articulate needs and thoughts, and relationships among students.

In fact, both principals and teachers speak of the profound impact these programs have had in promoting dialogue, thinking strategies, and authentic relationships among both students and faculty. The programs have enabled the staff to create more inclusive and responsive classrooms so that when a troublesome issue or conflict arises, the students and teachers have had so much practice in problem-solving they know how to converse in ways that address the problem. Particularly as a result of Caring School Community, there is a system in place for productively dealing with conflicts, differences, and problems within the classroom rather than having to rely on externally imposed solutions and sanctions.

The consistency of routines, the shared language, and the focus on positive relationships have reduced stress for students and faculty alike, increased the sense of safety and trust, and enhanced climate and morale despite the residual challenges of the pandemic. Teachers report that the Caring School Community program has laid the foundation for students feeling good about themselves, feeling that they belong, being able to express empathy for others, and knowing it's okay to make mistakes.

Meanwhile, staff express their perception that the schools' adults have become more aware of their own dysregulation and more knowledgeable about the strategies they can use to recenter themselves. The staff are devoting more time and effort to establishing, maintaining, and repairing relationships with students and each other. As a group, they have become more collective and less competitive.

The new mindset has also altered the way they talk about families and students. One school counselor framed the change in school culture as moving from judgment to empathy and curiosity. As one teacher pointed out, "community" and "community of learners" have become the big ideas in their classroom leadership and instruction. And community, viewed as a process of co-creation among students and adults, means giving voice to students and building on the rich diversity students bring to the classroom.

MIDDLE SCHOOL PROGRAMS

With the work on SEL solidly underway at the elementary level, staff considered undertaking a similar focus at the middle and high school levels. In 2019, as the elementary schools were beginning to implement Caring School Community, a group of middle school teachers and administrators discovered the CharacterStrong program.

This online program provides thirty-five weekly lessons, each lasting thirty minutes, for each grade level 6–8. The lessons focus on values and character traits such as gratitude, forgiveness, and patience and use videos, short activities, and class discussion to engage students in the topic. The goal of the lessons is to build skills to support students' sense of belonging and engagement as well as their overall well-being. Each lesson starts with an engaging relational activity that seeks to build community and connection between students.

After further exploration, the middle schools decided to use CharacterStrong as one component of their advisory program. The advisory program takes place for twenty minutes, four times a week, as an extended part of the second period, thereby engaging all teachers and students at the same time. At two of these weekly meetings, faculty deliver CharacterStrong lessons, spreading each thirty-minute lesson over two class meetings. At the other two advisory program meetings each week, faculty focus on AVID (Advancement Via Individual Determination) academic support lessons.

After the initial weeks of the CharacterStrong program, each lesson ends with a "character dare," in which students are challenged to use what they have learned by practicing a specific character trait during the following week. For example, in the lesson on gratitude, students are challenged to send a message to someone whom they are thankful to have in their lives. In the lesson on patience, students are challenged to let other people speak before they do. Each lesson provides multiple actions that students can take. In Corvallis's implementation of the program, the district has elected to have students discuss at the beginning of the next session the actions they have taken as a result of the previous session.

Although the design of this advisory program was well planned and the program itself had a productive start, the pandemic interrupted its implementation. As students returned to school in the fall of 2020, the middle schools strove to reestablish the advisory program. However, the lingering effects of the pandemic's interruption tended to draw teachers' time and attention to other matters and the effort fell short. Recognizing that the need still existed, in 2022 the district added support through a middle school curriculum coordinator who is charged with providing the same type and level of leadership that Amy Lesan offers at the elementary level.

In addition, the middle schools have initiated a program to promote a sense of belonging in the school and stronger connections between faculty and students. The "Four at the Door + One More" initiative involves teachers standing in the hall before class. The "Four at the Door" refers to (1) making eye contact, (2) making a physical connection, (3) making a personal connection, and (4) saying the student's name as each student approaches and enters the classroom. The "+ One More" means having an activity ready on the board so that when students enter the classroom they can get right to work.

AN APPROACH FOR THE HIGH SCHOOLS

The district's SEL approach at the high school level, Sources of Strength, began in 2016 with a suicide prevention grant. The Centers for Disease Control (CDC), which provides guidance on programs that address suicide, highlights Sources of Strength as the type of program that improves adaptive norms regarding suicide, connectedness to adults, and school engagement (Stone et al., 2017).

While Sources of Strength was initially developed as a peer leadership program for suicide prevention, it has evolved into a strengths-based, comprehensive wellness program that addresses suicide along with other issues such as substance abuse and violence. The program provides training for peer leaders and adult advisors in eight sources-of-strength areas that can promote self-awareness and resilience. The eight "protective factors" are family support, positive friends, mentors, healthy activities, generosity, spirituality, medical access, and mental health.

Unlike most suicide prevention programs that provide intervention only after an individual is in crisis, Sources of Strength focuses on developing the personal qualities that enable young people to cope with stress in positive ways that ward off even the formation of suicidal thoughts. The goal is to help students develop the resilience, emotional stamina, resistance, and courage to come through difficult situations with strength and positivity.

In that regard, Sources of Strength is preventative in its approach, rather than interventionist. The course provides students with an opportunity to share their feelings and help others who may be grappling with difficult circumstances. The program is designed to function as either a club or a course that helps students recognize the signs of stress and depression and become peer leaders for their school. It is important to note, however, that the peer leaders are not being trained to overtly intervene in other students' personal lives; they do not diagnose or recommend. Rather, the role of the peer leaders is to lead by example, demonstrating how they themselves handle difficult situations to achieve positive outcomes and helping to spread those strategies to other students.

Initially implementing the program as a club, the district and the high schools soon chose to provide resources for two sections of Sources of Strength to be offered as an elective course at each of the two high schools. At Corvallis High School, the course is taught by a highly popular physical education teacher and coach. He effectively creates a sense of community among students that enables them to learn more about themselves and their own sources of strength. The course culminates in a campaign led and operated by the class's peer leaders with the goal of uplifting other students at the school.

IN-DEPTH LOOK: CARING SCHOOL COMMUNITY AND COLLABORATIVE LITERACY

Both the Caring School Community and the Collaborative Literacy programs were developed by the Center for the Collaborative Classroom, a nonprofit organization. The origins of Caring School Community came out of refinements of the organization's elementary school Child Development Project (CDP), which was developed in the 1990s.

CDP was designed as a comprehensive at-risk prevention and social development program that integrated multiple elements and had as its goal the creation of caring and inclusive classroom communities that would foster a sense of belonging and responsibility. The component elements included weekly class meetings, cooperative learning activities integrated into social skill instruction, literature highlighting fictional and historical role models of prosocial behavior, cross-age helping and sharing activities, and developmental discipline.

CDP was piloted and refined in numerous school districts, leading to a second iteration of the program as Caring School Community. Caring School Community continues CDP's comprehensive quality but provides more manageable and better delineated structures and processes.

Caring School Community also retains the multi-element approach of the original CDP and continues to utilize a variety of structures and practices to build that key sense of community.

The program begins and ends the school day with morning and closing circles. The fifteen- to twenty-minute morning circles involve a greeting activity to ensure that every student knows every other student's name, a team-building activity, students sharing about themselves through a weekly student spotlight, announcements, and a review of the schedule for the day so that students know what to expect and can have a sense of agency. The closing circle is a short reflection time when students are invited to share an insight or experience from their past six or seven hours together. These bookends to the school day provide structure and foster relationships that build a sense of safety and trust, a home base within a caring community of friends.

In addition to these community-building meetings, there is a weekly class meeting so that students have an opportunity to discuss topics that help the classroom function more smoothly and resolve issues that emerge in the life of the classroom. The program provides well-delineated directions to help teachers facilitate these meetings as well as lesson plans around potential topics to cover. The issues can range from school life events such as preparing for assemblies, field trips, and a substitute teacher, to character-related subjects such as friendship, gratitude, and kindness, and to social issues within the classroom or school such as mean behaviors, unkind speech, resolving conflicts, and teasing.

To foster strong relationships among students and provide opportunities to interact with a variety of individuals, students are randomly paired with a different student each week. All students are paired with every other student in the class at some time during the school year. Teachers are guided to use these pairings during meeting times as well as during cooperative learning activities integrated into academic instruction. Using such processes as "turn to your partner," "think, pair, share," and "heads together," students engage in meaningful work with others, learn from differing perspectives, and develop relationships and the social skills to deepen them.

Caring School Community continues the buddies program from the earlier CDP as a way to build positive mentoring relationships. The buddies element of the program enables older students to demonstrate the social skills they have been learning while the younger students have the opportunity to work on learning activities with another student who has developed skills in that area.

The program also is designed to help students develop cross-age friendships, something that rarely happens given the grade-level structure of schools. The program's Cross-Age Buddies Activity Book provides detailed lesson options for teachers that touch on all curricular areas. The buddies lessons have academic content as a core element, but are designed so that students have fun and the opportunity to enjoy each other's company.

In addition to these components, the program includes weekly home connection activities that enable families to get involved around the theme of the week. The program also includes both class and individual tools for monitoring students' progress in developing social and emotional competencies. Principals receive a guide to schoolwide community-building activities that extend the sense of community in the classroom to the entire school.

Caring School Community also has a classroom management and discipline component focused on developing self-discipline through restorative practices that enable students to learn from their mistakes, repair the harm that has been done, and reenter the classroom community with dignity. The discipline guides for teachers and administrators provide strategies for addressing an extensive list of behavior issues including aggression, disengagement, disruption, exclusion, inappropriate language, social isolation, and others.

The comprehensive nature of Caring School Community provides students with a wraparound experience in which the structure, culture, and skills are aligned and consistent. From the start of the day to the end—through class activities, home connections, schoolwide activities, and even discipline—the thread of care, community, and skill development are woven together. Caring School Community's focus on students living the social skills they are developing on a daily basis and creating a culture of community is unique among SEL programs, with the exception of Responsive Classroom, which has a similar emphasis.

CASEL has rated Caring School Community as a SELect program based on the substantial evidence of its impact on students. The EASEL Lab's review of the program rates it highly, particularly in the area of social skill development. EASEL Lab reports that "Caring School Community is a K–8 program that builds classroom and schoolwide community while developing students' self-discipline and social and emotional skills" (Jones et al., 2021, p. 115).

The leaders at the Center for the Collaborative Classroom decided one more step needed to be taken to create the kind of experience that would effectively enable students to acquire the skills and knowledge to develop emotional resilience, healthy relationships, and improved academic performance. That step—to integrate social and emotional competency development into instruction—was based on their belief that *how* teachers teach matters as much as *what* they teach.

Given the importance of literacy in the elementary grades, the center's leadership team chose to design the Collaborative Literacy program so that it provides high-quality instruction in reading while incorporating instructional practices that foster social and emotional skill development. The organization's first work in literacy was done in partnership with the late Dr. John Shefelbine at California State University–Sacramento and culminated in the publication of Dr. Shefelbine's phonics program SIPPS (Systematic Instruction in Phoneme Awareness, Phonics, and Sight Words). SIPPS is now the intervention component of Collaborative Literacy.

Collaborative Literacy then launched a comprehension program titled Making Meaning, soon expanding with a writing program titled Being a Writer and a reading program titled Being a Reader. All three of these components have since been merged into Collaborative Literacy with the addition of phonics, word study, vocabulary, spelling, and handwriting.

Collaborative Literacy now possesses all the elements of a comprehensive K–6 English Language Arts program and utilizes instructional practices recommended by the National Reading Panel and the Institute of Education Sciences. The program includes such reading practices as shared reading, word study, read-alouds, guided strategy practice, individualized daily reading, and small-group reading.

However, embedded throughout the program's intentionally designed and fully articulated teacher guides are practices that facilitate development of social and emotional skills as students move through whole-group, small-group, paired, and individual instructional experiences. In fact, an entire section of each teacher manual is devoted to explaining the importance of facilitating social and emotional development as part of the teaching of literacy, as well as the specific social skills that are addressed in the curriculum.

That section begins by stating, "Helping students to develop socially and ethically, as well as academically, is part of the educator's role, and we believe it should be integrated into every aspect of the curriculum" (Center for the Collaborative Classroom, 2021, p. 22). Social development objectives for each week are identified in the teacher manual.

Teacher notes, classroom management notes, facilitation tips, and cooperative structure icons throughout the margins of the teacher manuals are guides to times when the teacher uses such strategies as "turn to your partner," "think, pair, share," and "heads together." Not only do the notes indicate when to use these strategies, but also how to debrief the strategies with students so that they are learning to refine their communication and collaboration skills. This facilitation enables students to develop more complex skills they can use in the future. For example, learning to listen to others evolves over time into building on one another's thinking.

In Collaborative Literacy, similar to Caring School Community, students are put in randomly selected pairs each week so that they can practice their developing skills with a different person. Just as in Caring School Community, the goal is to develop a sense of community through a common goal of proficiency in reading and writing, while enabling each student to pursue their own path to that goal.

In addition, the classroom libraries provided as part of the program reflect a diversity of authors, cultures, and characters and encourage discussions of social and emotional themes that provide modeling as well as problem-solving opportunities for students. Woven through every year of the program are readings and activities that help students think about and reflect on five core values—responsibility, respect, caring, fairness, and helpfulness—that emerge in the life of the classroom as well as in the literature students are reading. Other values such as courage, perseverance, gratitude, and compassion also arise as literary themes that teachers are guided to highlight and discuss with students.

Although there may be other commercial and nonprofit curricular programs that integrate some social and emotional competency development, Collaborative Literacy is unique in its thoroughness, depth of integration, and guidance for teachers. When used in conjunction with Caring School Community, it creates a seamless developmental experience for students.

PROGRAM EFFICACY AND OUTCOMES

Given the interruption and disruption created by the pandemic, it has been difficult for Corvallis to accurately assess the impact of these programs. The district uses the Youth Truth survey for students in grades 3 and above, but that instrument provides only general feedback. The district also uses Aperture Education's Devereux Student Strengths Assessment (DESSA) as a screener for students who are struggling with social and emotional issues. Elementary principals report that they are seeing improvements in reading on their internal reading assessments. However, the pandemic set back testing scores in reading and math across the state, making any comparisons with pre-pandemic years problematic and essentially invalid.

Extensive evaluation research on the Child Development Project revealed that it had a very powerful impact on students' academic and social skills and that impact continued well beyond the elementary school years (Schaps et al., 2004; Solomon et al., 2000; Watson et al., 1997). The change in title from CDP to Caring School Community reflected the most significant conclusion of the evaluation research—that creating caring and inclusive classroom and school communities where students experience a sense of belonging and efficacy and develop caring relationships with other students and adults is the critical factor in improving students' academic and social well-being.

At this point, no national evaluation studies appear to have been conducted on the social-emotional components of Collaborative Literacy, although the program uses strategies that are consistent with those that have been found effective in Caring School Community.

Corvallis selected CharacterStrong and Sources of Strength as its secondary programs. Neither of these programs is on CASEL's list of evidence-based programs for SEL. However, Sources of Strength is involved with a number of research partners, qualifying it to be included in the National Registry of Evidence-based Programs and Practices of the federal Substance Abuse and Mental Health Services Administration.

The developers of CharacterStrong indicate that the program is meant to teach empathy, emotional understanding, and regulation skills, as well as support character development through lessons about goals, habits, values, and purpose. The program design is intended to cultivate leadership and teamwork. The one randomized trial conducted on the program found that it enhanced academic engagement and perceived school safety. Teachers reported higher levels of safe behavior and school administrators reported improved attendance (Zhang et al., 2021).

An independent evaluation of Sources of Strength found that peer leaders could have a significant impact on the entire student population by increasing positive perceptions of adult support and the acceptability of seeking help (Wyman et al., 2010). Program implementation varies across sites with most schools forming extracurricular clubs to raise awareness about adolescent suicide and the prevention resources that are available.

Sources of Strength has received national attention and support. The Centers for Disease Control published a technical assistance package that featured Sources of Strength as an evidence-based, peer-normed program that could impact adolescent suicide. The Suicide Prevention Resource Center, the American Foundation for Suicide Prevention, and Substance Abuse and Mental Health Services Administration (SAMHSA) of the U.S. Department of Health and Human Services have listed Sources of Strength as a best-practices program in suicide prevention.

IMPLEMENTATION INSIGHTS

The size of Corvallis, both the district and the community, facilitates environments where the superintendent and central office administrators can get to know the staff and students. It's a size where leadership can have a powerful influence not only on the direction of the district but also on individual staff members.

One of Corvallis's strengths is the connection that central office leadership has on the ground in schools and classrooms. Superintendent Ryan Noss's commitment to social and emotional development is evident throughout the district as he attends SEL professional development, participates in learning walks, and meets with principals. The same can be said of Amy Lesan in her leadership of the elementary program and of the district leaders for the middle and high schools.

When principals and teachers talk about their SEL efforts, they echo the perspective that Superintendent Noss articulates about humanizing the work in schools—personalizing it and building communities in which people care about each other. Administrative vision, support, and presence matter in moving SEL programming forward in Corvallis.

Superintendent Noss has also provided the necessary support to ensure the programs' success. In a time of fiscal constraints, he consistently has allocated sufficient resources to purchase the programs, along with funds for ongoing professional development to further deepen teacher experience and expertise.

He has also designated responsibility to the program directors for each level to be leaders of this work and has committed resources to extend program coordination to the middle school level. His longevity as superintendent and the support provided by the district's school board constitute strong endorsements of his vision and reflect the board's confidence in the leadership he is bringing to the work in SEL.

In addition to administrative vision, leadership, and support, the district's long-term investment in professional development, particularly at the elementary level, has made a significant difference in the depth and consistency of implementation. Providing professional development time for Caring School Community and Collaborative Literacy has involved district professional day workshops, PLC time during early release days, learning walks with principals, an on-call liaison from CCC to address questions and concerns, and the development of internal teacher leadership to extend the district's professional learning capacity.

These resources were activated not just to launch the programs but to extend and deepen implementation over six years. That investment has made an enormous difference in teachers' capacity to deliver on the design and intent of the programs.

The elementary level benefited further from the selection of programs that are not only strong evidence-based programs in their own right but are also mutually supportive of each other. Caring School Community and Collaborative Literacy have common philosophies, language, instructional strategies, and community-building structures. It is easy for teachers to flow from one program to the other during the day. The programs' congruence also provides consistency for students, making it easier for them to align their performance with the anticipated structure of the day and to focus on learning.

The adoption of Bridges in Mathematics furthered that consistency so that the majority of the teacher and student day has a clear set of expectations, routines, instructional approaches, and rhythms. These predictable patterns have had a beneficial impact on teacher performance and school culture as well as on student learning.

What is also clear is that programs matter. Caring School Community and Collaborative Literacy are well-designed and well-articulated programs. The teacher guides are professional development in and of themselves. Both programs have been tested, evaluated, and refined by the Center for the Collaborative Classroom to ensure they are delivering on their promise. Both provide extensive professional development and ongoing supports so that teachers are better able to deliver the curriculum. As a result, teachers and administrators feel comfortable and confident in implementing the programs with fidelity, knowing they will achieve the desired results.

In particular, the emphasis on classroom and school culture and on embedded instructional strategies as a vehicle for developing social and emotional competencies advances teacher practice beyond delivery of a set of lessons to thinking about how the classroom functions to best support students' social, emotional, and cognitive development. Shifting the focus to how the classroom is structured to support community-building, positive relationships, and learning from mistakes moves teachers away from fixing students and toward fixing the environment.

When belonging, respect, and relationship matter in the classroom, the culture becomes strikingly different and far more supportive of student success. It also revitalizes teachers who entered the profession largely because of their love of children and, as Superintendent Noss says, humanizes the experience of school.

Clearly, no district initiative is perfect and the work at the elementary level continues to need refinement as new teachers enter the district and as some teachers are still challenged by the changes. The district's work at the secondary level reflects the challenges faced by many districts. There is a plethora of programs but disappointingly few that have the kind of pervasive impact as can be found at the elementary level.

The middle school's initiatives around CharacterStrong as an advisory curriculum and Four at the Door + One More as a way to personalize relationships between teachers and students are valuable. They are at an initial stage and teachers are still adjusting to them. The question is whether these initiatives will change the culture or embed social and emotional development practices into instruction when teachers see their mission as teaching the content of their subject and may not recognize or accept their responsibility for fostering social and emotional growth as well.

In the same way, Sources of Strength has been effective nationally as a suicide prevention and strengths-based mental health approach. Its focus on resiliency and peer leadership is a positive program model. That the district has endorsed the course as part of its curricular program is an important step in supporting the social and emotional development of the students involved in the program. However, its impact on the overall school community is less pervasive and it has little impact on the teaching practices of the other teachers at the school. Sources of Strength is perhaps most accurately viewed as a positive step forward but not a whole-school solution.

Clearly, progress monitoring of SEL is an area that will require further development in Corvallis.

CONCLUSION

Corvallis has made significant inroads in its implementation of programs focused on the development of social and emotional competencies. The consistent focus on SEL as a major element of its core elementary programs is having a profound impact on students as well as on staff. The strong base the district has built and the professional learning systems that are in place will only deepen and extend the impact for years to come.

When it comes to achieving the full mission of public education, administrative vision and leadership matter, as does the attention to professional capacity-building. But what stands out about Corvallis, what is absolutely fundamental to the district's effectiveness, is its leaders' unwavering commitment to classroom and school culture and to the understanding that a deep investment today in relationships and community will pay untold dividends in supporting students' social, emotional, and cognitive development for a lifetime.

Chapter 9

Building for Sustainability

*Cleveland Metropolitan
School District (Ohio)*

On October 1, 2007, Eric Gordon joined the Cleveland Metropolitan School District (CMSD) as the new chief academic officer (CAO) assigned to tackle the district's poor academic performance. At the time, CMSD was one of Ohio's worst-performing school districts. Ten days later, a fourteen-year-old student entered his high school, shot two students and two adults, and took his own life. That tragedy changed the direction of CAO Gordon's work and, as a consequence, the long-term improvement of education in Cleveland.

Eugene Sanders, the chief executive officer (CEO) of CMSD at the time of the incident, committed to increasing security and putting metal detectors in schools. However, he said the shooting was not a hardware problem, but rather a "humanware" problem that required the district to take a much closer look at the human circumstances that lay behind acts of aggression and violence.

In addition to taking steps to improve security, he believed the district needed to devise ways schools could proactively intervene to prevent these acts. He delegated that task to the new CAO, who formed a Humanware Department to lead the charge. To give the new department significant authority, Gordon positioned the leadership of the department at the executive director level.

David Quolke, president of the Cleveland Teachers Union, shared the concerns about teacher and student safety as well as an interest in addressing the humanware problem. He brought the union in as a partner to the initiative and designated Jillian Ahrens, one of the union's vice presidents, to co-lead a humanware executive committee with the humanware executive director. When Sanders left the district in 2011, Gordon was selected to take on the CEO position. With strong commitment to SEL from the school board, Gordon has continued to actively lead the SEL work across his twelve years as CEO.

CLEVELAND'S CHALLENGES

The task of proactively intervening to prevent violence has been a daunting one. Cleveland was a thriving commercial, industrial, and manufacturing center for much of its history through the mid-twentieth century. However, changing economic circumstances, new technologies, and the movement of manufacturing to southern states and other countries produced a significant economic decline beginning in the 1960s, leaving the central city with extremely high levels of poverty and unemployment that have continued through today.

The 2020 census identified Cleveland as having one of the highest child poverty rates in the country for cities of over 100,000 residents. With 46.6 percent of its children living in poverty, it was only slightly behind Syracuse, Rochester, and Detroit. In September 2022, Cleveland's unemployment ranked second in the nation among major metropolitan areas (Statista Research Department, 2022).

Educational improvement has also been a challenge. Fifty percent of Cleveland's adult population have just a high school diploma or less and only 18.6 percent have earned a bachelor's or graduate degree. Complicating the task for the school district has been the flight of students—particularly the children of white and economically advantaged parents who remained in the city—to charter and non-public schools. In 2022, CMSD enrolled approximately 36,000 students—only 54 percent of Cleveland's school-age children. Of those 36,000 students, 63.8 percent are Black, 17.2 percent are Hispanic, 14.5 percent are White, and 4.5 percent are other races. In contrast, the demographics of the charter and non-public school student population is 31 percent Black, 7 percent Hispanic, 53 percent White, and 9 percent other.

These figures mean that over 70 percent of Cleveland's Black and Hispanic students attend the public schools while fewer than 25 percent of Cleveland's White students remain in the public schools. Of CMSD's roughly 36,000 students, 23.2 percent are enrolled in special education programs, 13.1 percent are limited English proficient, 3.8 percent are homeless, and the poverty rate among students is so high that the entire district is classified as economically disadvantaged.

However daunting the task has been, the transformation in CSMD's educational performance over the past decade has been dramatic. Four-year graduation rates increased from 52.2 percent in 2011 to 80.9 percent in 2021, then declined to 74.3 percent in 2022 due to the pandemic. The increase in graduation rates for Black students rose from 22.8 percent in 2011 to 80.9 percent in 2021 and for Hispanic students it rose from 23.3 percent to 84.9 percent. In 2019, CMSD was ranked as one of Ohio's fastest-improving school districts with grades K–3 literacy improvement among the top 15 percent of districts, improvement on Ohio's performance index growth among the top 4 percent of districts, and graduation rate growth among the top 1 percent of districts.

In addition to enhancing academic results, the district's initiatives have also impacted safety and discipline measures. The past decade has seen decreases in disciplinary incidents, serious safety incidents, out-of-school suspensions, expulsions, and the over-identification of students of color for special education services. In the district's Conditions for Learning student surveys, students' perceptions of safety, support, and social-emotional capacity of peers have steadily improved.

The district's strategic plan included multiple initiatives that contributed to these results. Yet CEO Gordon and others in the district credit a good deal of the progress to the work they have done to enhance the climate and culture of CMSD's schools and the social and emotional development of its students.

EVOLUTION OF SEL PROGRAMMING IN CLEVELAND

Cleveland's SEL story is one of methodically building programming over time and setting up the structures and processes to ensure long-term sustainability. Eric Gordon began his education career as a math teacher and later, as CEO, brought to CMSD a strong focus on accountability. He also brought a systems approach to the work of school improvement, believing that each district is characterized by an ecosystem of curriculum, instruction, school climate, staff development, infrastructure, parent and community partnerships, and data to guide progress.

To sustain change means impacting and aligning all the elements of the system. That alignment begins with information to drive the system and then moves forward with the curriculum and programming that enable the district to achieve its goals.

Mr. Gordon also brought with him a longstanding belief that schools must educate the whole child and that social and emotional development is critical to academic performance. Once it was clear that humanware would be the focus of the work ahead, he and Cleveland's mayor reached out to the American Institutes for Research (AIR)—a research and development company that has done extensive work in the areas of accountability and social and emotional development as well as in violence prevention and school safety.

AIR provided a team led by Dr. David Osher to help diagnose the problems and provide recommendations. The specific task assigned to the AIR team was to determine what could be done in Cleveland's schools and by its mental health and other community agencies to improve the connectedness that students have to school, as well as their mental wellness and safety.

After nine months of interviews, focus groups, on-site observations, and analysis of data from the Youth Risk Behavior Survey and the administration of AIR's Conditions for Learning survey, AIR presented its findings. The team pointed to many strengths within both the school system and the county's public and private support system, particularly noting the commitment and dedication of district leadership, administrators, teachers, and collaborating community partners and foundations. However, AIR also identified significant gaps and problems in prevention programming, zeroing in on three in particular.

First, AIR identified eight factors that "place children and schools at risk for poor school outcomes, emotional and behavioral problems and disorders, violence and an absence of effective interventions to address these risk factors" (Osher et al., 2008, p. 13). These factors included the following:

- Chronic poverty and its impact on children
- Lead poisoning and lead effects
- Harsh and inconsistent approaches to discipline

- Reactive and punitive approaches to school discipline
- Unclear and inconsistently implemented disciplinary codes
- Poor adult supervision and role modeling in schools
- Limited family-school connection
- Schools where the mental health needs of students overrun the capacity of schools (Osher et al., 2008, pp. 13–15)

Second, AIR found "poor or weak conditions for learning exist in many Cleveland schools, along with an absence of effective approaches to improve these conditions" (Osher et al., 2008, p. 15). The results from the Conditions for Learning survey pointed to significant concerns among students around safety, connection, and support from adults, and the social and emotional skills of peers.

Third, AIR noted the schools' abilities "to address the factors that place children and schools at risk of poor outcomes and to improve the conditions for learning, teaching and development are undeveloped and inconsistent" (Osher et al., 2008, p. 17). There was a limited capacity to respond to warning signs and risk factors, an insufficient capacity to focus resources, variable quality in mental health services both in schools and in the community, and a lack of data systems to track needs, focus resources, and monitor progress.

AIR's almost two-hundred-page final report detailed ten general recommendations and fifty-six supporting recommendations. The ten general strategies follow:

Strategy 1: Improve capacity to assess, plan, deploy, and monitor humanware resources.

Strategy 2: Improve school procedures, protocols, policies, and practices.

Strategy 3: Improve school climate.

Strategy 4: Provide positive behavioral supports and social-emotional learning.

Strategy 5: Develop warning and response systems.

Strategy 6: Enhance school-agency collaboration.

Strategy 7: Enhance family-school partnership.

Strategy 8: Provide focused professional development and support.

Strategy 9: Focus funding agency resources.

Strategy 10: Collect and analyze key data for monitoring, evaluation, and quality improvement. (Osher et al., 2008, pp. 71–115)

The findings of the report and the concern generated by the school shooting sparked districtwide motivation to take action—and the district responded, maintaining its relationship with AIR to help facilitate the initiative. CMSD formed a partnership with the Cleveland Teachers Union (CTU), setting up an executive committee composed of district and union leaders, co-led by the humanware executive director and Jillian Ahrens from the union. Bill Stencil, who was the manager of the Office of Psychological Services at that time and would later lead the Humanware Department, played a key role on the executive committee in leading the districtwide prevention efforts launched as part of the humanware initiative. The district also formed a larger action team of about thirty individuals that included representatives of the mayor's office, central office department leaders, and community leaders to help steer and move the initiative forward.

Reflecting the seriousness of and commitment to the initiative, the executive committee met almost weekly, and the action team met monthly. Signaling the district's continued dedication to student well-being, these two committees were still meeting in 2022, although less frequently.

In 2008, the district began administering the Conditions for Learning survey to provide formative data to schools and district administrators on students' perceptions of safety, support, and social-emotional learning. At first it was administered once a year, later moving to two and then three times a year. CMSD adopted the SEL PATHS (Promoting Alternative THinking Strategies) curriculum with the pledge that it would be taught in all pre-K–5 classrooms by the classroom teacher.

The curricular adoption was phased in across two years with a professional development program that provided two days of training for all two thousand elementary administrators and teachers. Less intensive training was also provided to social workers, nurses, school psychologists, paraprofessionals, school bus drivers, and school secretaries to ensure consistency in approach across all staff in each school.

District leadership expanded the Humanware Department to include seven full-time coaches to provide support for PATHS during the first two years of implementation and then added other staff to support additional humanware initiatives. AIR was contracted to evaluate the implementation of PATHS and reported that "the implications of our findings include the hopeful result that despite the many challenges faced by this complex urban school district, and even with imperfect implementation and uncertain fidelity, student outcomes improved" (Faria et al., 2013, p. iv).

Over the next several years, the district took a number of interconnected steps. It joined CASEL's Collaborating District Initiative in order to learn from the SEL experiences of other urban districts. It tightened school security, procedures, and protocols. It abandoned in-school suspension rooms and converted them into "planning centers" staffed by planning center instructional aides (PCIAs) who could provide support and counseling. Planning centers were not just for referrals but were a place where students could self-identify as needing a break and a chance to talk to someone. In elementary schools, the planning center model was coordinated with the PATHS curriculum to create a common language across levels of intervention.

The district mandated that every school develop a student support team to provide faculty with an avenue for identifying actions to assist students potentially at-risk. It also convened rapid response teams that could provide interventions when schools were facing particularly challenging student circumstances. And, last but certainly not least, the district embedded social-emotional learning goals into its strategic plan and school academic achievement plans. All this was accomplished in spite of limited increases in education funding over the years.

Working hand-in-hand with the teachers union was critical. To more effectively support these steps, the district collaborated with the CTU on memoranda of understanding to support many aspects of the initiative and also worked with the CTU during contract negotiations to embed wording in the union contract to ensure the longevity of SEL approaches.

The current teacher contract requires a joint Humanware/Social-Emotional Learning Committee composed of equal representation from the district and the union. It includes sections on student support teams, discipline alternatives, planning center intervention programs, SEL-related class meetings for all ninth graders, and the student advisory committee. It mandates an SEL coordinator for each building, defines that coordinator's functions, and specifies a pay differential for the person serving in that role.

In addition, the contract requires that "all students in PreK–12 will have access to evidence-based, high quality SEL curriculum" (Cleveland Teacher Union Contract 2021–24, p. 81). The contract continues by adding that "schools will use district-provided SEL curriculum (e.g., PATHS, Second Step, Facing History) unless the school . . . selects from a menu of high-quality, evidence-based SEL curriculum programs approved by the Humanware Executive Committee" (Cleveland Teacher Union Contract 2021–24, p. 81).

This management–union collaboration not only ensured that the plans were well designed to meet the needs of teachers, but also, through the union's endorsement and leadership, enhanced buy-in from faculty in adopting the PATHS and other SEL curriculum and supporting the other changes being made throughout the district.

To give students a greater sense of agency and voice, the district engaged students in a "Not on Our Watch" (NOW) anti-bullying campaign and a "Winning Against Violent Environments" (WAVE) conflict resolution initiative. In addition, district leader Gordon convened a four-hundred-member student advisory committee, drawing eight to twelve students from each high school, and met with them four times a year to discuss issues of significance to students and the district. All of these initiatives continue currently.

In 2014, when AIR was asked to return for a follow-up assessment of what had been accomplished, the research team members reported that of the fifty-six recommendations offered in the 2008 report, ten were fully implemented, thirty-five were partially implemented, and ten showed no progress. Based on the Conditions for Learning survey, AIR also found significant improvement in the areas of student perception of physical safety, student support, and peer social and emotional competencies (Osher et al., 2014, p. 2).

The SEL initiative, however, did not stop there. As Eric Gordon describes, "It was a deliberate effort to build out an entire ecosystem that considered the information we need to drive the system, and then the curriculum and programming that gets us to our goals. What's interesting is that we did what we could do when we could do it, and then worked to fill in the gaps. So, it was spotty about how and when we filled those in."

In 2015–2016, the district adopted the Second Step program, developed by the Committee for Children as its middle school SEL program, to be delivered in language arts classes on a weekly basis. In 2016–2017, CMSD launched a major equity and inclusion initiative as well as a focus on adult SEL. The district piloted self-care programs for staff in yoga, mindfulness, and other strategies to address stress and further their personal skill development.

In 2018–2019, the district began working with the organization Facing History and Ourselves to provide professional development to all high school social studies faculty so that they would be able to integrate SEL strategies into their classroom instruction. That same year, the district also began examining the implementation of restorative practices.

Say Yes to Education, a national nonprofit organization committed to dramatically increasing high school and college graduation rates for inner-city youth, became a district partner. As a result of support from Say Yes to Education, 2019–2020 saw the start of a four-year phase-in of adding a family support specialist to every school in CMSD. These family support specialists provide families with assistance connecting with social, health, and legal services and build strong connections with families in their school.

In addition, the district has worked with out-of-school providers to include SEL as part of their programs. For example, New Bridge is one of those providers and describes itself as "a trauma-informed SEL learning center." New Bridge is funded by the district, Say Yes to Education, and local foundations to provide after-school programming in the studio arts in eleven schools, with local artists offering programs in painting, photography, crafts, and the performing arts. Programs are free to students and approximately eight hundred students are in attendance daily.

Using the Seven Habits SEL curriculum, each New Bridge after-school session begins with forty minutes of connection circles that focus on identity, executive functioning skills, and relationships. All the site coordinators and program instructors receive SEL training and have a monthly SEL objective and cultural focus. The program uses a shortened version of the DESSA (Devereux Student Strengths Assessment) to monitor students' SEL progress.

Throughout this period the district has promoted a conscious shift in language to reflect both a positivity about students and a service orientation among administrators and staff. Instead of saying "students" the district refers to them as "scholars," and instead of "parents and guardians" the district addresses them as "families and caregivers." Academic superintendents became "network support leaders," budget analysts became "financial partners," specialists became "barrier breakers" and "action team coaches," assistant principals became "deans of engagement" or "curriculum instructional specialists," human resources staff became "talent team members," and humanware coaches became "humanware partners."

All members of each school's staff, including clerical staff, custodians, and nutrition services personnel, as well as teachers and administrators, are considered to be educators, embodying the concept that every adult has a role in supporting the growth and development of CMSD's scholars.

The pandemic interrupted the district's SEL implementation. However, CEO Gordon and the humanware staff believe that their long-term investment enabled them to get through the pandemic with far less chaos than other urban districts experienced. As the pandemic waned and students re-entered their classrooms, SEL assumed a renewed focus.

"Whole human learning focused on student and educator social, emotional, cultural and physical wellness" is one of the four cornerstones of CMSD's "Vision for Learning in a Post-Pandemic World." The 2022–2026 Post-Pandemic Strategic Plan includes the goal to "strengthen and expand the implementation of current SEL efforts both for scholars and educators to meet all whole human needs," with additional investments in restorative practices and partnerships with out-of-school providers.

Four of CMSD's twelve core beliefs and guiding principles include that learning and teaching "integrates SEL practices naturally and is maximized by strong relationships," "happens through peer collaboration and conversation," "affords opportunities to explore others' perspectives and needs," and "incorporates restorative practices." The profile of a CMSD graduate includes being a skilled collaborator, exhibiting social and cross-cultural empathy, and being skilled at critical thinking and problem-solving—all SEL-related skill areas.

To move forward with this vision and the strategic plan, the Humanware Department and the humanware management–union executive committee are planning to provide a professional development refresher class for all elementary faculty in PATHS and for the middle school teachers involved in delivering Second Step, as well as continued professional development for high school teachers through Facing History and Ourselves—plans that were interrupted by the pandemic. In the interim, the department continues to offer voluntary professional development in PATHS and Second Step, as well as training for all new teachers.

A few factors have compromised the fidelity of the district's SEL implementation over the past several years. The Ohio Department of Education has strongly encouraged that all schools implement Positive Behavior Intervention and Support (PBIS) programs, which has shifted the focus from PATHS and other SEL initiatives to a system that emphasizes extrinsic rewards more than intrinsic social and emotional development.

The postponement of PATHS refresher training for all teachers has meant that some teachers haven't received training since the initial years of implementation in 2008 or 2009. There has not been refresher training in Second Step since its adoption in 2015. With a steady turnover in school principals over the years, new principals have entered the system without the experience, motivation, and training that enabled the district to move rapidly forward in the early years of the initiative. However, all new teachers do receive training in PATHS or Second Step, the deans of engagement and the PCIAs receive ongoing professional development, and any teacher is welcome to attend the continuing professional development in these programs. A number of Cleveland's schools remain national models for the PATHS program; still, the emphasis and attention given to PATHS and Second Step have faded for some schools and teachers.

On the positive side, the collective impact of all the SEL initiatives put in place by the district and the concentrated focus on data related to school climate have produced marked gains over time in the Conditions for Learning survey. For grades 2–4, perceptions of safety, adult support, and social-emotional capacity of peers continued to climb through 2018 and have remained stable since then. In grades 5–8, perceptions of safety, adult support, and social-emotional capacity of peers climbed slowly through 2019 before leveling off and declining post-pandemic.

Similarly, the high school has continued to see small gains in Conditions for Learning results throughout the past decade, with some decline due to the pandemic. Given that SEL programming for the high schools has begun only recently, it may be that scholars' earlier experiences with SEL programs in the elementary and middle grades had a long-lasting impact and carried forward into the high school years.

SELECTION OF SEL PROGRAMS IN CLEVELAND

To understand Cleveland's implementation strategies and the district's ability to sustain effective fidelity to SEL programming, it's important to take a close look at the programs the district has chosen to use. After a review process involving teachers and administrators, CMSD selected two explicit SEL skills instruction programs: PATHS for grades pre-K–5 and Second Step for grades 6–8. CMSD's schools follow a pre-K–8 model, so both programs are implemented in each of these schools. Both programs are CASEL SELect programs that have a strong evidence base and a long history of use across the country.

CMSD began its work on high school programs a few years after its pre-K–8 work was underway. The district partnered with the Cleveland office of Facing History and Ourselves to provide professional development in instructional approaches that all high school teachers could use to support students' social and emotional development. The Facing History curriculum is also one of CASEL's SELect programs.

PATHS for Pre-K–Grade 5

The PATHS curriculum has shown effectiveness in promoting social competence and reducing aggressive behaviors. Each grade has between thirty-six and fifty-three fully scripted thirty-minute lessons that are delivered two to three times a week. Some lessons may take longer than a thirty-minute session, depending on the needs of the students in the class. The lessons involve discussion, activities, role playing, and other active engagement strategies.

The areas of focus for the curriculum are self-control, emotional understanding, positive self-esteem, relationships, and interpersonal problem-solving skills. However, the major emphasis, as noted in the EASEL Lab's review of PATHS, is on emotional knowledge and expression (Jones et al., 2021, p. 290).

As Mark Greenberg and Carol Kusché, the university-based researchers who developed the curriculum, explain, "When emotional awareness is not sufficiently emphasized in SEL programs, children can model optimal problem-solving skills as a cognitive exercise, but do not utilize them when strong emotions are experienced during real life experiences. Children must be able to effectively regulate their emotional arousal and accurately process the emotional content of a situation in order to successfully employ cognition to solve a problem" (Kusché and Greenberg, 2011, p. 439).

For example, in the early grades, lessons touch on emotional understanding through feeling charts and cards so that students can name the emotions they are experiencing. The curriculum uses the stoplight graphic that encourages students to stop, think, and plan before acting. In planning their responses, students are encouraged by the curriculum to ask questions such as "Is it safe?" and "Will I be breaking any rules?" and "Will I be treating others the way I want to be treated?" The curriculum uses a turtle puppet to introduce the strategy of "turtling" to promote self-control, in which students withdraw into their shell to calm themselves and reflect on how to respond before coming forward with a response. Children's trade books are integrated into the program to illustrate particular social and emotional skills.

In addition to the lessons that provide explicit social and emotional skills instruction, the curriculum encourages teachers to generalize the lessons throughout the school day through ongoing complimenting, stories, and teaching sharing as a positive pursuit. Teachers are guided to create interactive environments of respect, caring, and empathy where the needs and feelings of others are considered. The curriculum also includes supplemental materials for parents so that families can apply in the home the instruction that is occurring in the classroom.

Second Step for Grades 6–8

As one of the first of the direct instruction social skills programs, Second Step was originally developed for elementary schools. Implemented in districts across the country, it is still the most widely used program for both tier-1 and tier-2 students.

Initially focused on empathy development and interpersonal relationships, the program used photos of social situations and role plays to help children understand the feelings of various individuals in the situation and to examine ways that children could be a positive actor in helping either resolve the situation or assist those in need. It encouraged understanding and managing emotions, being aware of the emotions of others, taking the perspective of others, and developing problem-solving and responsible decision-making skills.

Over the years, the program expanded in depth and range of social and emotional skill development, moved online utilizing videos instead of photographs, and extended to the middle school grades, still maintaining the interactive nature of the lessons.

The format of the middle school program is for the teacher to deliver one twenty-five-minute lesson each week that includes the illustration and practice of an SEL skill through partner and small-group activities, with follow-up activities that can be delivered throughout the week. The middle school program focuses on four major topic areas at each grade level with six or seven lessons in each area.

The topics include (1) mindsets and goals—which supports the development of a growth mindset; (2) recognizing bullying and harassment—which helps students to understand the impact of bullying and harassment and to identify prevention and intervention solutions; (3) thoughts, emotions, and decisions—which helps students identify, manage, and learn from strong emotions; and (4) managing relationships and social conflict—which supports the development of perspective-taking and conflict resolution in order to maintain healthy relationships. Each of the units ends with a performance task that calls on students to demonstrate the skills they have learned.

For districts that have advisory programs, there is an advisory guide with lessons on class meetings, class challenges, service projects, and advisory activities. The evaluation studies of the program confirm that Second Step promotes growth in social-emotional competence, executive functioning, and maintaining healthy relationships, while reducing problem behaviors (Jones et al., 2022).

Both PATHS and Second Step make professional development available and both indicate that the curriculum materials themselves serve as professional and personal learning for teachers as they read through the introductory and pre-teaching materials and then teach the lessons.

As explicit skill instruction programs, both provide depth in supporting students' skill development. However, as with any direct skills instruction program that requires time set aside to deliver the program, the determination and commitment of the district to sustain the allocation of time in the schedule and to provide professional development for new teachers and refresher training for veteran teachers is critical.

Although that commitment was evident at the initial implementation of these programs in Cleveland and was sustained for a number of years, the pandemic, other competing pressures on schools, and the lack of refresher training have diminished the fidelity of implementation of both programs. Whether the refresher training being planned for them by the Humanware Department will reignite fidelity of their implementation is an open question. This vulnerability exists not just in Cleveland but in any district that focuses on explicit skill instruction programs for SEL.

In spite of the decline in formal fidelity, a number of schools remain national models for PATHS implementation. District and school leaders believe that the prior years of experience with these programs have changed how teachers approach instruction, class management, and relationships with students. Teachers with experience in the programs have continued to use particular lessons at appropriate times and focus on the development of social and emotional skills in the way they teach. District leaders believe that this change in how teachers approach instruction is one of the reasons that the Conditions for Learning survey continues to show modest but positive gains.

Facing History and Ourselves for Grades 9–12

Facing History and Ourselves is a nonprofit organization founded in 1976 and noted for developing powerful social studies and English language arts curricular materials that address issues of bias, prejudice, and intolerance. Using historical cases such as the events leading up to the Holocaust, the origins of the Armenian genocide, and the school desegregation conflicts in Little Rock, Arkansas, the materials raise important social and ethical issues by focusing on identity and group membership and how those factors may influence the human potential for prejudice, passivity, complicity, and destructiveness.

Through an in-depth study of a historical case, students have the opportunity to reflect on the human vulnerabilities that enable and further intolerance and, as a consequence, to consider their own prejudices and beliefs. By examining the role that identity and group membership serve among the perpetrators, bystanders, and upstanders in these cases, students also strengthen their ethical reasoning and develop a stronger sense of moral courage.

The instructional practices embodied in the materials are designed to present multiple perspectives, promote engagement and reflection, foster empathy and moral reasoning, and complicate students' thinking so that they won't accept simple answers to complicated problems (Berman, 1997). These instructional strategies also support student voice and agency and build a sense of community within the classroom as students collectively work to appreciate differing perspectives, understand complex issues, and build on each other's thinking.

The U.S. Department of Education's former National Diffusion Network listed Facing History as an exemplary program. Today, it is one of CASEL's SELect programs based on the evidence that it enhances empathy, prosocial behavior, and classroom climate. The EASEL Lab's recent review of secondary programs found that it was one of only four of the eighteen programs the lab reviewed that had a strong focus on providing culturally competent SEL. In fact, the lab found that Facing History "incorporates culturally responsive teaching practices that promote student identity development and engagement with students' lived experiences" (Jones et al., 2022, p. 116).

CMSD had worked with the Cleveland Facing History office over the years to provide professional development for social studies and English language arts teachers. A number of CMSD high schools offered a Facing History and Ourselves elective course. The district also launched a project-based high school named Facing History New Tech; it is attended by approximately two hundred students and incorporates a Facing History course into each grade level.

In 2021, the district asked Facing History to provide professional development for all high school teachers from all subject areas in instructional strategies that would promote the social and emotional development of high school students. All high school teachers, in small groups, received a ninety-minute professional learning experience that presented them with a set of instructional strategies and resources to help them focus on SEL through an equity lens.

Through discussions on the role that identity and group membership play in providing a sense of belonging and in making choices, the session focused on how teachers can build stronger relationships with students, provide them with opportunities for voice and agency in the classroom, and help create a culturally responsive and inclusive classroom community. For example, one strategy illustrated how teachers can work with students to formulate a classroom contract around norms that best support the learning of all students.

The most significant goal of the professional development was to shift the teacher's role to that of facilitator of an inclusive classroom community. To accomplish that goal, teachers were provided with strategies that promoted engagement and belonging and nurtured social skill development. Teachers received a resource bank of classroom strategies and administrators received a look-for checklist to support teachers in their implementation of the strategies.

A ninety-minute session for all teachers isn't adequate to provide consistency in approach at the high school level. However, CMSD continues to contract with Facing History to offer follow-up sessions for interested teachers and provide support to schools interested in initiating Facing History elective courses, case study units, or advisory programs. Although the implementation process is still in its early stages, CMSD administrators perceive that Facing History's professional development fosters a pedagogical approach that supports students' social and emotional wellness and can be applied in all high school courses.

PROGRESS MONITORING: CONDITIONS FOR LEARNING SURVEY

One of the key leverage points in Cleveland's SEL implementation strategy has been the use of AIR's Conditions for Learning survey. AIR initially used the survey in its assessment of the issues facing the district after the 2008 shooting incident. Eric Gordon's belief in the value of data to enable progress monitoring and continuous improvement of initiatives and to leverage the fidelity of implementation moved the district to sustain the survey's administration across the past fifteen years.

The survey was initially administered once a year but soon expanded to three times a year. Formative data reports were provided to principals and other administrators along with targets for excellence for every school. In 2018, the district shifted to two administrations of the survey each year and expanded it to include data on students' perceptions of self-regulation in the areas of inhibitory control and attentional control.

The Conditions for Learning survey incorporates three scales that are directly related to social-emotional development. The first is students' perceptions of safety, which encompasses physical and emotional safety as well as students' sense of whether their school has a safe and respectful climate. Applying a scale of *strongly agree* to *strongly disagree*, the survey asks students in grades 5 through 8 to respond to such descriptors as "Most students in my school treat each other with respect," "I sometimes stay home because I don't feel safe at school," and "Students at this school are often teased or picked on." Students also rate how safe they feel outside around the school, in the halls and bathrooms, and in classrooms.

The second scale examines students' perceptions of adult support, focusing on how much students feel listened to, cared about, and helped by teachers and other adults in the school. The scale for grades 5–8 includes such indicators as "My teachers really care about me," "Adults in this school are usually willing to make the time to give students extra help," and "The teacher for this class notices if I have trouble learning something."

The third scale is labeled social and emotional learning and measures students' perceptions of their peers' social and problem-solving skills. This scale's survey for grades 2–4 asks students to answer "yes," "sometimes," or "no" to such items as "Most students in my school stop and think before they get too angry," "Most students in my school do their best, even when their school work is hard," and "Most students in my school do their part when we work together on a group project."

The survey offers a fourth scale that examines students' perceptions of the challenge level of the material they are studying. However, the district concluded that students tend to equate "challenging" with their own inability to do the work, thereby confusing their personal frustration with the rigor of the content matter and making the feedback from this scale not particularly useful.

The reports given to each school not only include the school's scale scores as compared with the district and subgroup breakdowns, but also the results on each individual question. The reports end with suggestions for moving forward to improve the conditions for learning. The depth, frequency, and continuity of the data over time have given the survey significant meaning within the district, enhancing the staff's motivation for moving SEL efforts forward. The survey results are used as a metric at senior leadership meetings and in supervisory meetings with principals. The effective use of the survey data may be one of the reasons that SEL has been so effectively sustained over time.

STUDENT VOICE

Superintendents in numerous other districts have formed student advisory councils and even had students serve as ex-officio members of school boards. However, launching a four-hundred-member student advisory committee in an urban district is truly an exceptional feat. Eric Gordon has not only formed that council but has engaged and empowered students in providing meaningful and valuable information to the district.

Each of the thirty-one high schools selects between eight and twelve students, with at least two per grade, to serve on the advisory committee. The schools are asked to reach beyond the typical student council representatives and to select students who represent the diversity of groups in the school. The student advisory committee meets with the CEO four times a year. In forming the meetings' agendas, CEO Gordon insists that the council engage in meaningful dialogues that provide valuable information on issues of significance to the district. Known for telling the Humanware planning staff, "If we know the answers, we don't have to ask the questions," he personally leads and facilitates every three-hour student advisory committee meeting.

The issues CEO Gordon raises with the student advisory committee are serious ones and have important implications. For example, when in-person instruction resumed in 2021–2022, poor student attendance was jeopardizing academic performance. He turned to the committee to help administration understand why attendance had fallen off so significantly and what the district might do to enable and encourage students' return to school.

Then, in 2022, Cleveland's newly elected mayor sought the district's help to address youth violence. CEO Gordon brought that issue directly to the student advisory committee in a series of meetings, resulting in a student representative from each high school meeting with the mayor to offer insights and recommendations.

By having such a large student committee and asking the members to weigh in on significant issues, CEO Gordon is sending a message to the high school students in Cleveland that their voice matters. He views student voice and agency as essential elements in the development of social and emotional skills, as well as a means of fostering an empowering environment in the district's high schools.

INSIGHTS FROM CLEVELAND'S IMPLEMENTATION

Sixteen years of sustained focus on SEL in a district with so many competing concerns and circumstances represents an exceptional commitment and an unwavering belief in the value of SEL for moving the district's academic and school culture goals forward. For Cleveland's leadership, both in administration and in the union, strong SEL programming is foundational to achieving progress in any area of the district's work.

Across those sixteen years, there has been a remarkable stability in leadership. Mr. Gordon will have led the district's work in this area for four years as CAO followed by twelve as CEO. Bill Stencil has been part of the leadership of the Humanware Department since its inception, eventually taking over as executive director; although he will retire at the end of the 2022–2023 school year, he has provided continuity across the many years of the district's SEL work. Jillian Ahrens, who remains a vice president in the union, continues to cochair the monthly management–union executive committee. AIR provided intensive support and facilitation in the early years of the initiative and remains as a valued external advisor, as well as supporting the Conditions for Learning survey. The mayor's office experienced continuity in both the tenure of the mayor himself and the tenure of his education leadership staff. That kind of constancy in an urban district is rare and has led to stability in direction and commitment around the growth and development of SEL initiatives.

CEO Gordon is moving on from CMSD at the end of the 2022–2023 school year, but he has put in place a solid infrastructure for sustaining SEL programming well beyond his tenure. SEL is embedded in the vision, mission, strategic plan, and other policy documents of the district. An entire department with extensive expertise is devoted to SEL programming, embedding the work into the infrastructure of the district. The assessment systems for the district include progress monitoring of SEL.

Many of the SEL initiatives are written into the union contract, including SEL curricula, an ongoing management–union committee to lead the SEL work, SEL building coordinators, student support teams, class meetings, and the student advisory committee. There is strong school board support for SEL, and it is likely the board will look for a similar commitment to SEL as they consider candidates for the next CEO. Having that degree of embeddedness has sustained SEL programming across a decade and a half and provides foundational support for its future.

Eric Gordon's emphasis on accountability and the leveraging of the Conditions for Learning survey have been highly effective in ensuring that schools and school-based administrators take SEL seriously. Combined with ongoing professional development in SEL curricula for new teachers and strong coaching support from the Humanware Department's staff, these factors have enabled the district to sustain both the use of SEL curricula and the schools' planning centers.

The leveling out of growth on the Conditions for Learning survey may, in fact, be due in part to the lag in providing both refresher training for all veteran staff in PATHS and Second Step and initial training for new school administrators. With the interruption caused by the pandemic and the pressures of recovering from students' learning loss over that time, there is diminished emphasis on SEL curricula in schools. In addition, students returned to school from the pandemic with increased trauma and needs, which could also be impacting the Conditions for Learning results. A key takeaway from this experience is the necessity of sustaining professional learning and renewed training in basic programs at periodic intervals.

As with other districts implementing SEL, having a solid infrastructure to support growth and development has been critical. The Humanware Department, led by someone at the executive director level, is not only an important affirmation of the district's commitment but a key asset in facilitating the work. The humanware partners who serve as coaches to the district's schools and other staff who support various initiatives are valued resources that provide continuity and foster depth in programming.

The teachers union in Cleveland is a strong one, as it is in many urban districts. The union contract itself runs 276 pages in length, indicating attention to detail and the expectation of involvement. Partnering with the union from the beginning has been a significant asset in strengthening CMSD's SEL initiatives. That partnership has meant that teachers viewed various SEL initiatives as being endorsed by both their union representatives and administration. It offered greater credibility and authority and produced a firmer commitment among teachers to follow through and implement these initiatives with fidelity.

Leveraging community partnerships has also been an important asset in moving SEL forward. Working with New Bridge and Say Yes to Education to support SEL programs in out-of-school settings, as well as in the family support specialists' outreach to families, has fostered consistency in students' experiences and expectations.

The district has selected SEL programs that have depth and the demonstrated ability to produce results. The district has also been thoughtful about ensuring that there are programs to support tiers 1, 2, and 3 in the MTSS (multi-tiered systems of support) framework. However, PATHS and Second Step require setting aside time in the schedule to provide direct instruction in social and emotional skill development. Although both are designed to influence the overall culture of the classroom and have follow-through activities that extend across students' school day, they are vulnerable to seeming like just another subject to teach—one that isn't on the required state tests—rather than part of a comprehensive approach to building a holistic learning community.

It takes sustained and vocal commitment from district leaders to hold school-based administrators and teachers accountable for maintaining instruction in these programs in the face of pressure to use the time on basic reading and math skill development that is on the state tests. That some schools remain deeply committed to SEL implementation and serve as national models of PATHS implementation is a sign of the deep ownership that school-based administrators and teachers have taken for sustaining programs at a high level.

Because of the focus on subject area expertise, implementing SEL programming at the high school level has been a challenge for most districts. That is the case in Cleveland as well. The ninth-grade class meetings and Facing History's continued professional development have been of some help in building community, but have not yet provided a comprehensive intervention at the high school level.

It also takes regular and ongoing professional development to maintain and grow teacher skill in delivering these programs. When those factors lag, the quality and consistency of implementation falter and the programs may even be abandoned over time. Given the after-effects of the pandemic and the upcoming transitions in leadership, CMSD is facing a critical moment in its evolution of SEL programming.

CONCLUSION

There is much to learn from an urban district that has been working to implement SEL for more than fifteen years. What stands out is that the district took a painful incident and sought to find ways not only to heal but to prevent such incidents in the future. In doing so, they set in motion a process that has evolved over time and continues to do so. Each year, as Eric Gordon has said, they did what they could and then looked to the future as they strove to fill in the gaps.

Looking back, district leaders believe that they should have devoted more time at an earlier point to working with adults—especially teachers and administrators—on their own social and emotional competencies. They also say that they probably delayed too long in providing refresher SEL courses as professional development for all staff. Identifying those gaps is a first step in addressing them and the district is taking proactive steps in both areas. In the meantime, CMSD's leaders have put key elements in place that bode well for the continued expansion and deepening of SEL in the district—and for the social and emotional development of the students entrusted to their care.

Chapter 10

Promising Practices at the Secondary Level

Success in SEL programming has been much greater at the elementary level than at the secondary level. In the traditional self-contained elementary classroom, teachers spend much of the day with their students and have the opportunity to create the kind of inclusive and caring community that supports social and emotional development. They also can build in time for weekly direct instruction in specific skills that are then discussed throughout the week or as relevant occasions emerge in the life of the classroom.

SEL at the secondary level presents a particularly perplexing problem for school districts. All the case study districts described in this book experienced this challenge. Given the subject area specialization at the secondary level and the more limited time that an individual teacher spends with a class, it is problematic to create an environment that replicates the elementary experience. Secondary teachers, particularly at the high school level, tend to focus on subject-specific curricula, which makes building a consistent approach to SEL across a middle or high school much more difficult.

Some teachers are reluctant to accept responsibility for social and emotional development because they see as their primary focus the subject-area standards and learning targets required by state accountability tests. And some feel unprepared or inadequate to address social and emotional issues or skill development.

Even when secondary teachers express interest in SEL, they soon discover a dearth of evidence-based programs at their grade level. While some elementary SEL programs such as Responsive Classroom,

Caring School Community, and Second Step extend into middle school, very few programs exist at the high school level.

As the secondary program evaluation completed by Harvard's EASEL Lab points out (Jones et al., 2022), these programs tend to be "aged-up" versions of elementary programs that substitute teenage characters for elementary-age characters but maintain the same content. The programs can feel condescending, inauthentic, and uninteresting to teens who are dealing with much more complex issues.

For high schools in particular, Jones and her colleagues emphasize the need to shift the developmental focus of SEL programs from such middle-school salient domains as conflict resolution and emotional knowledge and expression to a more mature focus on healthy relationships, responsible decision making, and ethical values.

The EASEL Lab researchers also found that very few of the secondary SEL programs adequately address equity issues. Combined, these factors explain why all of the case study districts struggled to find ways to address SEL at the secondary level.

At the middle school level, advisory programs have emerged as a primary vehicle for delivery of SEL instruction and for building a sense of community among students. For example, Corvallis's advisory program provides the time for all teachers to offer the CharacterStrong program. In schools that have retained the middle school model, organizing students and teachers into teams promotes greater consistency in their approach to SEL. It allows for team-based planning among teachers, enabling them to collaborate on SEL instruction and team-wide community building among students.

However, financial constraints have forced many districts to move away from the middle school model, returning to a junior high school model in which students are no longer organized into teams with a core set of teachers, and where teachers instead teach multiple grades in their subject area. Some of these schools offer advisory programs that include SEL, while others have delegated SEL instruction to be included in a particular subject area.

Cleveland, for example, integrates Second Step into language arts classes. Other districts have relegated the direct instruction of SEL to health classes. Marshalltown strives to engage all teachers in the Capturing Kids' Hearts program by promoting the development of classroom norms through class contracts and through relationship-building strategies such as greeting students individually at the classroom door.

There has been greater success using these strategies at the middle school level than at the high school level. Generally, high schools are larger and more diverse. Teachers are more focused on their subject areas and less willing to take minutes from the limited time they have with students to focus on SEL. However, several strategies have emerged that have proved to be productive in promoting social and emotional development at the high school level.

HIGH SCHOOL ADVISORY PROGRAMS

The first of these strategies is a high school advisory program that organizes all students into small groups that remain together with one or more faculty members across their four years in high school. Advisory program meetings vary in frequency from a couple of times a week to several times a quarter. For example, Naperville's advisory program involves two meetings each week.

Advisory programs serve multiple purposes in addition to building a sense of connection to school and a sense of community among students in a larger high school. They enable advisors to monitor progress, attendance, and other elements of their advisees' school experience. They provide time for grade-level meetings, discussions with counselors, and co-curricular activities. They also enable a school to implement an SEL advisory program. In some cases, as in Naperville, the SEL curriculum is district-generated. Other districts have adopted advisory curricula from such organizations as Engaging Schools, Facing History and Ourselves, and EL Education.

The most significant challenge in implementing advisory programs at the high school level is developing the commitment of the faculty to deliver the curriculum with fidelity and meaning. The variability in both commitment and capability often compromises the effective implementation of advisory programs. Effectively supporting advisory programs requires intensive professional development, collegial support, and a commitment to including this activity in teachers' professional responsibilities and evaluation outcomes.

SOCIAL-EMOTIONAL LEARNING TARGETS

A second strategy emerging from the case studies involves requiring all teachers to identify a social-emotional learning target as well as an academic learning target for each lesson. Naperville is exemplary in its implementation of this strategy. Several conditions were present in Naperville that supported this approach.

The district compiled a set of social and emotional learning standards that teachers could reference as they developed lessons and organized their instructional practices within the lesson to facilitate academic as well as social and emotional development. The district also required that teachers post both their academic and social-emotional learning objectives in the classroom and discuss them with students so that students were clear about the learning targets for the lesson. In addition, teacher practice included student reflection on the learning targets at the end of the lesson so that students were monitoring their own progress and the teacher was receiving feedback on the efficacy of instruction in achieving the targets.

In some cases, Naperville teachers who taught the same subject came to a common agreement about the specific social-emotional learning targets they were going to address in particular lessons as well as across an entire course. In other cases, whole departments spent time identifying which targets would be addressed within which courses. Although the social-emotional learning targets were not on the high school report card as they were at the elementary level, the teachers' involvement produced greater ownership of these targets by the faculty, and SEL was more deeply integrated into instruction.

Although this strategy requires SEL standards and the determined integration of learning targets into lesson design and delivery, it constitutes a powerful vehicle for integrating SEL into daily instruction at the high school level.

A COURSE DEDICATED TO SEL

A third strategy for effectively pursuing SEL at the high school level is to offer Facing History and Ourselves or a similar program, particularly targeting all ninth-grade students. Cleveland's insights around the value and impact of Facing History's courses and instructional strategies have been confirmed by such districts as the Hudson Public Schools in Massachusetts and the Jefferson County Public Schools in Louisville, Kentucky. Both districts created a ninth-grade required civics course that featured curricula from Facing History and Ourselves (Berman, Chang, and Barnes, 2012). The courses used historic cases of prejudice and intolerance to help young people examine issues of injustice.

In Hudson, the course examined the history leading up to the Holocaust through a Facing History and Ourselves curriculum titled *Holocaust and Human Behavior*. In Jefferson County, the course focused on the civil rights movement in the United States through another Facing History and Ourselves curriculum titled *Choices in Little Rock*. In both districts, the courses included group and individual service-learning projects that enabled students to make a difference on an issue of personal concern.

Traditional curricula in social and emotional skill development may not be as compelling to high school students as they are to younger students. Facing History overcomes that barrier through courses and curricular material that engage students in meaningful and deep learning and conversations about what it means to be a bystander or upstander in the face of injustice. The curriculum uses emotionally powerful material to raise important social and ethical questions while at the same time engaging students in individual and shared reflection, perspective taking, consideration of multiple points of view, and moral dialogue (Berman, 1997).

The courses enable students to reflect on their own beliefs and prejudices and develop a stronger sense of moral courage and civic commitment. Although the courses focus on historical events, because they deal with complex human emotions, identity and group membership, and issues of prejudice and intolerance, they are deeply meaningful to students' personal lives. The courses use the distance of history to provide perspective on the personal circumstances of the present. Because they emphasize perspective-taking, empathy, self-reflection, and critical thinking, they address pivotal areas of social and emotional development appropriate for teenage students.

The evaluation data on the impact of these courses are compelling. Lieberman (1991) studied the effects of Facing History courses and reported that participating students showed significantly higher development in perspective-taking and social-reasoning abilities. Bardige and Barr found that the courses enhanced students' interpersonal perspective-taking skills, moral reasoning ability, and ability to think about subject matter in complex ways (Bardige, 1988; Barr and Bardige, 2013). Schultz and colleagues (2001) noted a similar increase in moral reasoning and relationship maturity along with a reduction in racist attitudes.

Barr and colleagues (2015) observed that students reported greater civic efficacy, tolerance for others with different views, and positive perceptions of classroom climate. In a randomized control trial, Domitrovich and colleagues (2022) reported that the Facing History course resulted in high levels of empathy and prosocial behavior, along with stronger participatory citizenship beliefs.

Berman, Chang, and Barnes (2012) reported that in the cases of Hudson and Jefferson County, students came to see their school as a microcosm of society and recognized their own responsibility for creating a more just and compassionate school community. Because these courses dealt with such meaningful and compelling issues, they were highly engaging for students and effective in helping students take the next steps in their social and emotional development.

Over the years, the Facing History and Ourselves curriculum has received accolades from the EASEL Lab, CASEL, the U.S. Department of Education's former National Diffusion Network, and many others.

Although Cleveland doesn't offer a course to all students, the district offered professional development in Facing History's pedagogical methods, first to all social studies teachers and then to all high school teachers. The district also launched a Facing History New Tech High School structured on the principles and pedagogy presented in the program's course materials.

Offering a required Facing History course, or a civics course that integrates the Facing History curriculum, to all ninth graders has great potential for changing the climate and culture of a high school and the social and emotional skill development of students. By enabling students to confront issues of prejudice and intolerance, develop empathy and perspective-taking skills, and become upstanders for ethical and responsible decisions, these courses can help establish a positive and inclusive culture while building a sense of community and connection. They can form a foundation for the inclusion of the instructional strategies Cleveland sought to integrate into all high school classrooms. They can also foster a sense of community among students that can make advisory programs in the upper grades more meaningful.

BUILDING PROFESSIONAL CAPACITY

Cleveland's focus on a pedagogical approach that would impact all secondary classrooms is, ultimately, a powerful way to teach social and emotional skills at the secondary level. Although the training Cleveland provided secondary teachers was only an initial introduction to that approach, it highlights a vision of classrooms where inquiry, collaboration, engagement, and community enable students to practice and refine their social and emotional skills in the service of learning. It embodies but goes beyond the identification of a social and emotional learning target and views the way teachers teach and manage their classrooms as a collaborative learning community in much the same way as elementary classrooms have the capacity to create that kind of learning community.

The alignment between SEL and instructional practices will be discussed in more depth in the next chapter, but it is important to note that focusing on subject-specific content doesn't mean a teacher can't design instruction to be student-centered or can't facilitate the development of a sense of community in the classroom.

These three promising practices for reaching high school students—a core ninth-grade Facing History and Ourselves course, a schoolwide advisory program using SEL curricula, and social-emotional learning targets embedded into lesson planning—are not mutually exclusive. Together with student-centered and community-building pedagogical classroom approaches, they can provide a framework for an effective approach to SEL at the high school level.

Still, it is key to remember that no matter how strong a program or strategy is, and as challenging as professional development for a high school faculty can be, the bottom line is this: developing the professional capacity of faculty is essential for the delivery of a consistent and meaningful approach to SEL at the high school level.

Chapter 11

What Have We Learned?

Each district discussed in this book is unique in its size and demographics as well as in its evolution of SEL programming, choice of programs, and the way it has monitored progress. However, what the case studies reveal are fundamental strategies that have enabled these districts to succeed in their implementation. The reverse is true as well—implementation is compromised when these strategies are absent.

It is clear from these cases that there is no one best place to start. Much depends on context. The Cleveland Metropolitan School District, thrown into an urgent pursuit of solutions after a school shooting, undertook an independent analysis to diagnose what it needed to do. The Marshalltown Community School District, faced with changing demographics and environmental disasters, engaged in collaborative problem-solving as a way to shift districtwide thinking about how best to approach the growing diversity and adverse experiences among its student population.

The Corvallis School District found its way to SEL through a literacy curriculum adoption that resonated with teachers. Moriarty-Edgewood administrators felt compelled to respond to evidence of students' emerging needs in the areas of mental health and well-being.

On the other hand, SEL in Naperville Community School District 203 grew out of a community-based strategic planning process, and the district committed to a methodical approach grounded in the development of standards and learning targets. The Virginia Beach City Public Schools' journey to SEL emanated from its exploration of how to improve school culture and have all students feel known, valued, and included.

Although each district began at a different place with different motivations and program initiatives, their initial forays into SEL deepened administrators' commitment as they observed the contribution these efforts made to the well-being of students, the productiveness of instruction, and the positive learning environment fostered in schools.

Just as there is no one best place to start, there is also no one best program or road to success. These districts chose different programs to address unique needs and followed different evolutionary paths to deepen programmatic implementation. Some—such as Cleveland, Naperville, and Corvallis—pursued districtwide initiatives. Others—such as Marshalltown, Moriarty-Edgewood, and Virginia Beach City—chose to pilot programs that would then stretch to other schools in the district.

In some cases, the implementation efforts were methodical, in others they were more episodic. As CEO Eric Gordon pointed out regarding the evolution of programs in Cleveland, districts do what they can when they can and then fill in the gaps that emerge.

In each of these districts, implementation was a process of learning by doing and then building upon that experience over time. In each case, there was messiness to the implementation. Administrators looking back on their efforts cite multiple areas they wish they had addressed earlier. The jaggedness of execution and the filling in of missing pieces appear to be normal and consistent aspects of implementation. In fact, none of the districts' efforts documented here are complete. All are a work in progress. All have made some strategic errors and changed trajectories to address those errors.

Despite the differences in starting place, programming, and evolution of implementation, the experiences of these six districts offer important insights and commonalities that can serve as building blocks, guiding principles, and cautionary signs to support other districts' implementation efforts.

A SHIFT IN THINKING

One of the first building blocks that emerges from these case studies is that fostering social and emotional development in young people is best supported by a significant shift in thinking about how we approach educators' relationships with children.

Social and emotional development isn't facilitated by didactic instructional methods in social and emotional skills or by adult power and control in offering rewards or threatening punishment. Development is facilitated by deep listening and empathy, building trusting adult–child relationships, and creating caring and responsive classroom and school environments. The profound shift occurs when adults cease to view the child as the problem and instead realize that children do the best they can based on the experiences they've had and the skills they've acquired within the environments they've lived in or encountered.

As Stuart Ablon so eloquently points out, blaming and punishing the child doesn't expand their repertoire of skills. It only further stunts their development of lagging skills. Teaching skills requires seeing from the child's perspective, discerning how the child perceives the problem, and then working with the child to explore solutions. Those solutions may require the child to develop or refine particular skills, but they also may necessitate that the adults alter their own behavior or the environment in ways that best support the child's development.

Teachers and administrators will always have power and control in school situations. That's the structure built into educational systems. However, teachers can maintain order and project high expectations, confidence, and assurance without using dominance and coercion to control students. In fact, exerting authority rather than approaching situations with empathy, inquiry, and curiosity undermines trusting relationships and prevents students from processing and learning from their mistakes.

In today's rapid-paced classroom environment, given the pressure to produce results on time-sensitive learning targets, it is sometimes difficult to step back from our adult agendas and truly listen to the children in our classrooms . . . to observe them and understand how the culture and climate of the learning environment are facilitating or inhibiting their learning. Yet, it is taking that time to step back, reflect on the child's perspective, and make changes in adult response and classroom culture that best facilitates students' social and emotional growth and sense of well-being. It is those adult behaviors that lay a positive foundation for the implementation of SEL.

In the Marshalltown and Corvallis districts, it was the professional development in Collaborative Problem Solving that helped staff make that shift and laid the groundwork for much deeper work in social and emotional learning. In Moriarty-Edgewood, it was a districtwide focus on trauma-informed care and adverse childhood experiences that modified teacher and administrator perspectives. In Virginia Beach City, it was the professional development in Responsive Classroom.

In Cleveland, the depth of professional development in PATHS and the longstanding commitment to that program supported teachers as they adjusted their approach to students. And in Naperville, it was the extended work on developing standards, learning targets, and assessments in collaboration with CASEL.

In each district, exploration of issues of equity and diversity helped shift the classroom tenor from expecting students to adapt to the norms of the dominant culture to, instead, projecting an attitude of inclusivity toward culturally diverse norms and lived experience. The work in equity enables us as educators to appreciate that we should avoid pre-judging students' experiences, confront our own unconscious biases, and seek understanding through curiosity and inquiry. The work in equity focuses on changing our own behavior and the environment of the classroom and school to provide inclusive, identity-safe spaces for students where they can be fully present and grow.

And similar to the exploration of cultural diversity and equity, it has been professional development and practice in universal design for learning—initially emerging from work with students with special needs but now applicable to all learners—that is reorienting educators from viewing the student as having problems adapting to the curriculum to instead understanding that the curriculum itself has accessibility problems that require change.

Each of these approaches redirects the adult mindset from seeing the student as the problem to recognizing that the learning environment needs to change so that students can develop lagging skills and deeper understanding and have an expansive opportunity to grow socially, emotionally, and cognitively. As Coburn (2003) points out so clearly in her study of the Child Development Project, planning for SEL implementation requires considering teacher beliefs and attitudes and pursuing strategies that promote or enhance that consequential shift in thinking.

CULTURE EATS STRATEGY FOR BREAKFAST

Peter Drucker's oft-quoted phrase that culture eats strategy for breakfast certainly applies to the implementation of SEL. Creating a culture of community in the classroom and school is a prerequisite to effectively implementing any SEL program. The thirty-minute weekly SEL lesson is insufficient, even with extensions into the school day, unless the culture supports the social and emotional skills children are learning. No matter how strong the strategic plan, the experience that adults and children live each day in the classroom and school will dictate whether educators can deliver on the promise of social-emotional programs.

The enthusiasm for SEL among elementary-level faculty and administrators in Virginia Beach City, Corvallis, and Marshalltown derives from the change in classroom culture they experienced after implementing programs such as Responsive Classroom and Caring School Community. These programs focus on creating a sense of community within the classroom and building positive relationships among students and between adults and students. Community-building processes such as morning meetings, closing meetings, class meetings, partnering, and buddy programs serve to create a responsive, equitable, and inclusive culture.

Not only do these programs foster a sense of social and emotional safety, but they also enable students to feel known, acknowledged, and valued so that they can take learning risks, learn from their mistakes, and feel good about themselves. Through their day-to-day engagement with their peers, students feel connected to others; they develop empathy as well as a sense of responsibility for their actions.

The classroom community also fosters an appreciation for the richness of diversity in a classroom and the value that each individual contributes to the whole—enabling children to reach across and learn from differences, build constructive and positive relationships, and develop self-understanding and self-confidence through their sense of connectedness.

As studies of the Child Development Project showed, the sense of inclusive community creates an environment in which students live the social and emotional skills they are learning. This fact doesn't negate the productivity of direct instruction in social and emotional skills but rather provides a culture in which learning those skills has meaning and relevance. In fact, when done in combination, each delivery method can enhance the impact of the other.

The significant impact of community-building processes on students' and adults' social, emotional, and cognitive growth speaks to the necessity of using these strategies as first steps into the SEL arena. Actions speak louder than words, and experiencing a positive social and emotional environment has a deeper meaning than skill lessons alone. SEL programming isn't a check-off on a list of things to do but rather an environment and a way of being with children. Teachers are not just instructors of social skills but facilitators of community.

ADULT SEL MATTERS

In the six case study districts as well as in much of the social-emotional learning literature, an important insight emerges about the fact that school districts need to pay attention to the social-emotional learning and behaviors of the adults in the schools. Feeling an urgency to meet this need, districts have pursued staff reward and acknowledgement programs, special events to lift staff morale, and adult self-care and health and wellness programs.

Each of these strategies provides some relief and uplift to faculty but is unlikely to overcome the pressure and stress of addressing the diversity of student needs in overcrowded and underfunded classrooms. Although smaller class sizes and additional staffing supports are important systemic improvements, the most effective avenue for addressing adult SEL lies in helping adults better connect with their students and develop caring and responsive classroom environments that enrich everyone in the classroom, including the adults.

For example, during a visit to one of the districts in this study, a profound illustration of a supportive adult-student relationship was on display. Instead of modeling an SEL lesson from the curriculum the district was using, one third-grade teacher, who had been holding morning meetings throughout the year, turned to the class and asked them to explain to the visitor what it was like to be a student in this classroom. These third graders were eloquent in describing the sense of community they felt, the support they offered to each other so that all could learn, and the caring relationship they had with each other and their teacher. They offered concrete experiences as examples of each of these characteristics.

The teacher then added that the class was a source of strength for her, explaining that when her sister passed away suddenly in the middle of the school year, the students came together to express their caring and support at a time when she felt devastated by the loss. It renewed her sense of meaning for the work she was doing and deepened her connection with the children in her classroom. Just as she had provided a caring community environment where students could grow, the class had reciprocated in providing that same caring environment for her in a time of need.

When educators create that caring community environment in their classrooms and schools, it enhances adult well-being, reduces stress, and supports professional and personal growth. Administrators can help as well by modeling the development of caring and responsive school environments. They can apply the same empathy, inquiry, and curiosity to adult situations that we want teachers to apply to students' circumstances.

Building a sense of community in classroom and school environments is not an easy or quick solution. In truth, there is no quick fix for adult SEL. It requires time and a daily recommitment to building the professional capacities of adults and fostering authentic and collaborative relationships among staff, with the goal of collective efficacy and community around a positive vision of youth development.

PROGRAM QUALITY MATTERS

A plethora of SEL programs is commercially available and more come on the market every day. As the work of the EASEL Lab at Harvard points out, the various SEL programs have different emphases and utilize different instructional strategies. Discerning the good ones from the inadequate ones is a challenge, as is identifying which programs best address the particular needs and context of a specific school district.

In every case, when it comes to adopting programs, quality matters. When teachers experience a quality program, it builds their investment in delivering the program. Many of the programs adopted by the case study districts—Collaborative Problem Solving, Responsive

Classroom, Collaborative Literacy, Caring School Community, PATHS, Second Step—have served to strengthen the districts' implementation efforts because of the credibility the programs have with the faculty delivering them.

CASEL's evaluation of whether the program is evidence-based and has demonstrated an impact on students' skill development and behavior is clearly one important standard. However, that is only the initial base upon which districts should make judgments about programs. Another key indicator of quality is the program's depth.

A high-quality program is professional development in and of itself. It builds teachers' depth of knowledge and belief in the value of SEL and in the strategies for delivering it. It provides a solid rationale built on research in social and emotional growth. Quality programs engage students in reflecting on real issues they face without trivializing them or providing pat answers. They engage students in inquiry and problem-solving. Those that impact classroom culture make it easier for teachers to teach and build relationships between teachers and students and among students.

High-quality programs also focus on students appreciating the intrinsic rewards of connection and personal growth rather than external rewards of praise or accumulation of tokens. Word-of-the-month and skill-of-the-week programs may be simple to execute but have limited value other than for vocabulary development.

Meaningful programs involve serious engagement in the subject matter through empathic role playing, problem-solving conversations, and the posing of multiple solutions. Skill development doesn't come from a box or an online curriculum; it comes from dialogue and practice in situations that are relevant to the students' experience.

Quality programs are often more challenging to implement. They call on teachers to spend more time reflecting with students as they process and seek to understand differing social and emotional strategies for dealing with situations. They may also call on teachers to change some of their instructional approaches, ways of communicating, and disciplinary strategies. However, they also will have a deeper and longer-term impact on the growth and development of students and on teacher practice. When the districts in these case studies took full advantage of a program's depth, their implementation was more successful.

PROFESSIONAL LEARNING MATTERS EVEN MORE THAN THE PROGRAM

Success in implementing SEL within the districts in these case studies was largely dependent on the structures and professional development processes put in place to provide teachers and administrators with depth in professional learning. Virginia Beach City not only provided multiple levels of week-long trainings in Responsive Classroom, but it also created a Responsive Classroom Academy to further support teachers in learning and sharing practices. Cleveland provided full-day trainings in PATHS to the entire elementary faculty, as well as coaches to support teachers' classroom practice.

Naperville phased in its implementation with three years of online and face-to-face professional development and also trained peer leaders in each school. Corvallis provided ongoing, embedded professional learning, classroom walk-throughs, and professional learning communities, and is training teacher leaders in each school. Marshalltown is supporting faculty through multiple levels of week-long trainings in Responsive Classroom practices and is developing the in-house capability to provide ongoing training and support for Collaborative Problem-Solving.

Although Moriarty-Edgewood is just beginning its trek along the SEL path, the most significant emerging need has been quality professional development that goes far beyond the online support provided by its chosen program. The professional development that is needed and being provided by these districts extends across multiple years and includes the training of new teachers as they come on board.

It's easy to assume that teachers and administrators, based on their love of children and desire to teach, have the interpersonal and intrapersonal skills to promote social and emotional development and develop a sense of community in the classroom. While some educators do have those skills, for many this is an area in which they have received little or no training and for which the "two-hour introductory workshop" is woefully inadequate.

As educational leaders, we would not simply hand teachers a teaching manual in reading or math, give them a short introductory workshop, and send them off thinking they will be proficient in delivering quality instruction. The same is true of helping teachers create culturally inclusive classroom communities that nurture social and emotional development or helping teachers provide meaningful instruction in social skill development.

Quality professional development in SEL goes beyond charting the sequence of lessons and explaining the delivery models for those lessons. Professional capacity to provide SEL entails helping adults learn to listen and observe carefully for lagging skills, facilitate community-building in the classroom, honor the diversity of student and adult cultures and lived experiences, resolve conflicts in constructive and instructive ways, restore relationships when there has been a transgression, reflect on the language they use in the classroom, support students in developing self-regulation skills, enable students to have voice and agency in the classroom and build on each other's thinking, and much more.

This is a tall order—and can seem overwhelming to teachers who are already faced with so many demands on their time. School and district leaders can support teachers by encouraging them to take small steps and to consider starting with an element that is already part of their classroom day.

One example is the powerful influence that teacher language and tone of voice can have on children and their social and emotional skill development. Sarcasm, judgmental comments, labeling, accusatory language, threats, and warnings can constitute painful micro-aggressions that make a deep impression on students, causing them to withdraw trust and be reluctant to take academic risks in front of their peers. Surprisingly, even praise that is used to control student behavior can have a negative effect on the very student voice and agency that teachers want to develop. While reflection on teacher language is just one facet of SEL professional development, it exemplifies the depth of professional development that best supports SEL implementation.

Professional capacity in SEL is not only associated with delivering the curriculum or facilitating social skill development as one builds community. It is also a reflection of our own social and emotional capabilities, which we must strive to develop to a high degree in order to effectively model them in the company of students. For example, how we approach and resolve conflicts in our personal lives creates behavioral patterns that inevitably are on full display in the classroom. Therefore, professional development in SEL sometimes means unlearning long-established behaviors, as well as developing new practices of adult–student and adult–adult interaction.

Time for quality professional development is sorely constrained and often relegated to infrequent professional days during a school year. Every district struggles with this dilemma. In the end, if a district wants to derive meaningful results from SEL, the district's leadership must identify SEL as a priority and allocate time and other resources accordingly.

The six districts in these case studies found creative ways to support summer institutes, release time, SEL coaches, professional learning communities, teacher leaders, learning rounds, and embedded professional learning. When districts ensured that teachers had the time and ongoing support across multiple years to implement programs well, the programs achieved greater depth, longevity, and teacher ownership.

It is teachers' professional capacity to deliver on program goals that essentially determines the success or failure of a program. Investing in teachers is critical to the success of SEL implementation and is not an area where a committed district can expect to cut corners.

LEADERSHIP STRUCTURES SOLIDIFY COMMITMENT

The case studies in this book demonstrate that the commitment of district leaders, particularly the superintendent, is critical. In all six sites, the superintendents had sufficient longevity in their positions to provide credibility, stability, and continuity in SEL programming, and they pursued specific actions to ensure successful implementation.

The first and most basic action was their vocal support for the importance of SEL in achieving a positive instructional environment, supporting student well-being, and enhancing students' academic performance. They also translated that vocal support into district policy through district vision and mission statements, strategic plan goals, theories of action, attributes in the profile of a graduate, and formal board policy statements. These actions created an embeddedness of SEL in the goals and direction of the district's efforts.

In addition, these superintendents and district leaders established an administrative structure to support implementation, designated responsibility to high-level administrators in their district, and provided sufficient district resources in terms of time and funding so that these leaders and departments could effectively execute their role. In Marshalltown, Corvallis, and Naperville, that responsibility was designated to an assistant superintendent for student services. In the larger districts of Cleveland and Virginia Beach, whole departments, cross-district teams, and/or dedicated district leadership groups were formed to facilitate implementation. The leadership of those departments and cross-district teams was integral to district SEL operations.

In each case, these leaders were given the means to support professional development, staffing for coaches, stipends for peer leaders, and other resources to ensure that implementation was successful. Also in each case, district leadership ensured that there was time in the school schedule to address SEL.

In the larger districts, these leaders invested in the development and provision of extensive online resource banks to support the development of professional capacity. Virginia Beach created its "stockpile" of SEL resources and activities. Naperville provided standards, learning targets, and instructional resources online. Cleveland supplied its teachers and administrators with extensive resources on its website.

All the case study districts ensured that teachers had leadership opportunities in the selection of materials, the provision of professional development, and the leadership of implementation at a school level. Each district involved teachers in selection and/or design of the SEL program. School-based teacher leaders were critical to implementation in Naperville, Cleveland, and Virginia Beach. Corvallis is in the process of pursuing that strategy as well. In Cleveland, teacher leadership extended to co-facilitation with the union and embedding that leadership into the teacher contract.

Building an infrastructure of administrative support for SEL, appointing an SEL leader who is given the resources and administrative and financial support to follow through on implementation planning, and enabling teacher leadership are essential to success in realizing district SEL goals.

In addition, consistent communication by administrative leaders to teachers, the board, parents, and the public about the importance and meaning of SEL addressed multiple purposes: it validated SEL's importance, helped people understand the role of SEL in enhancing student performance, and normalized SEL as a primary responsibility of educators. For example, communication from the superintendent in Virginia Beach in response to public attacks on critical race theory and SEL served to defuse the issue, reduce tension, and affirm the importance of the work the district was undertaking.

One other action that each of the district leaders took to support SEL implementation was to have their district join communities of practice so that their staff could learn from the experience of others and better support their internal efforts. Cleveland has been a member of CASEL's Collaborating District Initiative since CDI was formed in 2008. Marshalltown, Naperville, Moriarty-Edgewood, and Virginia Beach became members of AASA's SEL Cohort and the SEL Impact Project. Marshalltown networked with its area education association and surrounding districts to support the district's professional development in Collaborative Problem Solving. Corvallis networked with other districts implementing programs of the Center for the Collaborative Classroom and with a state SEL network.

These support networks host ongoing opportunities for superintendents and SEL leaders to meet and discuss important issues in implementation and to visit each other's districts to see programs in operation. In addition, several of the districts formed community-based networks of support—such as the mental health network developed by Marshalltown and the out-of-school-time network supported by Cleveland—to facilitate communication, collaboration, and consistency across contexts in support of students.

Each of these districts has had the benefit of consistent leadership over an extended period of time. However, changes in leadership are now on the horizon for Cleveland. Knowing that every district experiences a leadership change at some point, that inevitability must be taken into account through planning and preparation.

What CASEL (2021) found in studying its Collaborating District Initiative is that the emphasis on SEL and the continuity of implementation extended across changes in leadership of both the superintendent and board. In these CDI districts, leadership not only provided the structures that would ensure continuity but empowered ownership among administrators and faculty, who found significant value in the SEL programming they were implementing.

By consistently communicating the importance of SEL, building SEL into district policy documents, providing an infrastructure of leadership and support, allocating significant time and financial resources to support both SEL leadership and professional learning, and joining communities of practice networks, the six superintendents featured in this book's case studies helped ensure depth and continuity in their districts' implementation. Their visible and persistent commitment to seeing SEL meaningfully and consistently implemented has enabled these districts to be successful.

USING DATA AS A LEVER TO PROMOTE SUCCESS

Monitoring progress in facilitating social and emotional development and in implementing SEL programs has grown in importance, and the available tools have expanded significantly over the past decade. Most of the case study districts made effective use of these tools to move their SEL initiatives forward.

Cleveland's use of the Conditions for Learning survey across fifteen years of its initiative provided feedback to school and district leaders on students' experiences with safety, adult support, and social-emotional learning. Naperville's building an accountability system into the elementary report card called the attention of both teachers and parents to the importance of tracking social and emotional development.

Virginia Beach uses an adaptation of the Panorama Education survey to measure SEL skill development, student well-being, and students' sense of belonging. The data are provided to school leaders and teachers, along with tools to analyze their progress and reflect on the strategies they are using.

Corvallis uses the formative assessments built into both the Collaborative Literacy and Caring School Community programs to ensure they are reaching both academic and social-emotional learning targets. Several of the districts provide "look for" protocols as vehicles for reflection and feedback in administrative walk-throughs and collaborative learning walks.

Each of these districts uses a different tool to monitor progress, but all of them then apply the resulting information to leverage a continuous improvement cycle that advances implementation. By disaggregating the data by school, grade, and population, they are better able to engage administrators and faculty in dialogue about ways to improve results. And by making SEL data a part of the district's accountability system, they are validating its importance to the overall success in achieving district goals.

The one gap in these districts' use of data is the analysis of fidelity of implementation. The degree to which teachers fully utilize SEL strategies and programs in their daily instruction, plus the quality of their classroom implementation, are critical factors—both in students' success in acquiring social and emotional competencies and in the extent to which classrooms support a sense of community. However, as critical as these elements are, few districts have examined issues of fidelity and quality of implementation beyond the administrative walk-throughs, coaching cycles, and teacher learning walks that enable staff to reflect on implementation.

In part, the lack of analysis regarding fidelity of implementation may be due to the complexity of examining the reality of classroom practice, which would require ongoing classroom observation and analysis rather than self-reports. In part, it may be due to the lack of funding resources to pursue such a deep level of analysis.

In spite of the challenges, when that research is integrated—as it was in the studies of the Child Development Project—it reveals important insights into the impact of SEL on students, teachers, and the climate and culture of the school. It can also provide valuable information to administrators in planning next steps in their SEL programming.

ALIGNMENT CHALLENGES

Corvallis's work in aligning its instructional pedagogy, discipline methods, and social-emotional learning principles is a powerful reminder that SEL programming works best when such alignment is intentionally addressed. Particularly in its selection of elementary literacy and math programs, Corvallis found curricula that integrate SEL practices and model such SEL principles as learner-centered instruction, inquiry, and student voice and agency. The district's exploration of restorative discipline practices is also an attempt to bring consistency to a student-centered, whole-child approach.

The lack of alignment with instruction, classroom management, and discipline can undermine the positive impact of SEL strategies

(Berman, Jodl, and Barnes, 2023). When instruction is primarily didactic and teacher directed, it communicates to students that they are expected to remain passive and compliant, thereby undermining the kind of interactivity, community building, and problem-solving so critical to the development of social and emotional capabilities.

SEL shifts the focus from what the teacher is doing to what the students are experiencing. It supports student voice and agency by encouraging students to express personal perspectives and pursue individual questions and interests. Moving away from lecture, worksheets, and teacher-directed instruction and toward small-group discussions, open dialogue, collaborative problem-solving, and inquiry processes enables students to actively participate in the life and operation of the classroom and to refine their social and emotional skills in the context of the learning process.

Learner-centered instructional approaches encourage meaningful dialogue, careful listening, perspective-taking, and authentic relationships, all of which align with SEL curricula and learning targets and provide opportunities for students to demonstrate and enhance the social skills they are learning. Using cooperative and collaborative learning processes characterized by group heterogeneity and interdependence and supported by embedded social skill instruction, constructive feedback, and student reflection help integrate social, emotional, and cognitive learning and move instruction well beyond superficial group work. Not only do these processes strengthen the development of social and emotional skills; they also build a more productive classroom culture and help students derive meaning from the curriculum.

In the same vein, alignment with districts' diversity, equity, and inclusion (DEI) efforts is equally important. Because most teachers and administrators come from white, middle-class backgrounds, some may not be aware of the potential for inherent biases in their approach to social and emotional norms. Instead of overtly recognizing the rich diversity of students' cultural norms and cultural and racial heritages, they may use SEL lessons to project the social values, norms, and mores of the dominant culture.

It is critical that SEL draw upon the diversity of students and honor those differences in racial and cultural heritages. Students not only need to see *themselves* in the curriculum and in instruction; they also need to have a window onto the diversity of the *world around them*.

In order for students to feel known, valued, and included, they must feel that their classrooms and school are identity-safe and culturally responsive. Therefore, district SEL, culturally responsive pedagogy, and DEI efforts need to be coordinated and mutually supportive. Although they may be somewhat separate initiatives, they are grounded in the same principles of respect, authenticity, and positive relationships.

Each of the case study districts sought to coordinate their SEL and equity efforts. Naperville, for example, brought its SEL, multi-tiered system of supports (MTSS), and equity initiatives together under the umbrella of creating inclusive classrooms and schools. The DEI and humanware teams in Cleveland met together to plan next steps. Corvallis framed SEL as an integral part of its pursuit of equity, as did Virginia Beach and Marshalltown.

Alignment with discipline strategies is similarly vital. The goal of SEL-oriented discipline systems—whether developmental discipline, logical consequences, or responsive and restorative practices—is for students to learn from mistakes, master self-control, and repair and restore relationships. Exclusionary and punishment-oriented classroom management and discipline strategies can undermine students' social and emotional development by focusing on compliance and control rather than learning and relationships.

Even popular classroom and school management systems such as Positive Behavior Intervention and Supports (PBIS) may conflict with the goals of social and emotional development. By focusing on external rewards and compliance with adult expectations, PBIS's behaviorist approach can be effective in the short term at controlling negative behavior, which is why so many school districts have adopted this approach. However, PBIS operates from a completely different mindset about discipline and self-control and can detract from SEL's development of intrinsic motivation for learning.

Too often, PBIS and SEL are seen as two separate and independent systems—or worse, PBIS is viewed as an SEL program, thereby giving students mixed messages about adults' authenticity in supporting their social and emotional development versus simply wanting to control their behavior. In Virginia Beach, the educators working on SEL and PBIS consulted with each other to build bridges between the approaches; their goal was for PBIS to provide students with voice and agency, while responsive and restorative practices supported inclusion and community building.

Although SEL's alignment with instruction, culturally responsive practices, and discipline systems is important for providing students with a consistent and coherent school experience, this discussion tends to take place well after the initial implementation of SEL programming. As practitioners gain experience with SEL, they come to understand the depth and meaning of nurturing social and emotional competencies, and as they focus on building community in the classroom, the inconsistencies among practices become clearer. The leaders of SEL initiatives need to be conscious of this discordance and pursue forms of professional development that enable teachers to build consistency across their practices.

A MISSED OPPORTUNITY—SERVICE LEARNING

The National Commission on Social, Emotional and Academic Development clearly outlined community service and service learning as important SEL strategies for enhancing students' social and emotional development. Although many districts pursue these strategies, particularly at the high school level, the practices are often extracurricular and not integrated with the district's SEL initiatives. Few commercial SEL programs include service extensions with their SEL lessons.

Berman, Chang, and Barnes (2012) point out how the Hudson Public Schools in Massachusetts integrated service learning into all grades K–12 as part of its SEL efforts. Taking a different approach, the Jefferson County (Kentucky) Public Schools integrated service learning into its ninth-grade Facing History and Ourselves course so that students could experience the positive social and emotional development that is fostered by making a difference in their community. These service-learning experiences were transformative, particularly in urban and low-income areas, and empowered students to recognize that they had the skills and abilities to make a difference in their community.

Sociologist Helen Fein coined the term "universe of obligation" to represent the extent to which we feel a sense of obligation to care for and protect others (Fein, 1979). Service learning and community service opportunities enable students to expand their universe of obligation beyond family and friends, while applying the social and emotional skills they are learning to situations of need in their community and the world around them (Celio et al., 2011; Yorio & Ye, 2012).

Among the vulnerabilities of SEL programming is that it tends to be restricted to the dynamics between individuals and to be contained within the context of the classroom and the school (Berman, Jodl, and Barnes, 2023). Service learning and community service promote the same skills as are fostered by SEL programs—listening, perspective-taking, empathy, compassion, and collaborative problem-solving. Demonstrating how these skills are applied in real-world situations provides constructive learning opportunities that solidify students' understanding and appreciation of such skills.

For many school districts, including the ones documented here, the failure to incorporate service learning into the standard curriculum and into their SEL initiatives is a missed opportunity to support students' social and emotional growth and provide them with realistic and experiential practice of key relational skills.

CLOSING THOUGHTS

The purpose of this book is not to provide theoretical frameworks but rather to share the actual stories and practical insights from district-wide SEL implementation. As stated at the beginning of this chapter, what is clear about SEL implementation is that there is no one best path to follow nor one best program to adopt.

Instead, for those who would make progress, there is a layering of successful elements of change that lead to a deepening of fidelity to a vision. Implementation is messy and never takes place the same way in any two districts. Understanding a district's context and the opportunities and challenges that context presents is vitally important to the success of implementation. Many roads can lead to the same destination.

Still, these stories of districts' struggles and achievements provide snapshots of experience-tested strategies that promote success. One of the most foundational strategies is to understand that undergirding any SEL initiative must be the recognition that cognitive, social, and emotional development are inextricably linked and mutually supportive of one another. Ignoring any one of them compromises the others.

The social and emotional curriculum and culture of the classroom and school are the ground upon which cognitive development is staked.

This fact requires us to be as conscious in structuring that social and emotional curriculum and culture as we are in structuring academic instruction and curriculum.

District and school leadership not only have to recognize this truth but also communicate it to staff, parents, and the community as the reason that strong SEL programs are essential for students' academic success and social and emotional well-being. They must also convey to stakeholders that working to develop such programs is worth the investment of time, effort, and resources.

Because of the inextricable links among cognitive, social, and emotional growth, the most important point that emerges from these cases is that you don't get results by implementing skills-based instruction in SEL without also providing the programs and professional development that will transform the mindset of educators and the climate and culture of the classroom and the school. Providing children with the lived classroom experience of appreciating relationships with others; of possessing a sense of connection to an inclusive and culturally responsive classroom community; and of being known, cared about, and valued is the essential ground upon which cognitive, social, and emotional growth take place.

SEL isn't a thirty-minute lesson that you check off on a weekly schedule and assume it has accomplished its purpose. And SEL is not about fixing broken students. Rather it is about creating environments that foster personal and academic growth. SEL requires deep listening and building authentic relationships with and among students. It requires consciously and continuously reflecting on the classroom and school environment, on teacher practice, and on alignment with systems of instruction and discipline to best support growth and development.

The cases presented here reveal important elements in any SEL implementation strategy. Leadership matters in setting district priorities, establishing policies, building infrastructures of support, allocating resources, using data to monitor and leverage progress, and communicating to others the vital importance of SEL. Quality programs also matter, but even more important is the development of the professional capacity of staff to deliver on the promise of these programs. As Cynthia Coburn (2003) articulated, effective scaling of any implementation requires depth in teacher knowledge, belief, and ownership, which is only achieved through high-quality professional learning, ongoing refinement, and systems of support.

The case studies in this book reflect each district at a point in time. Although CASEL's evaluation of the CDI districts demonstrated that the commitment to SEL can be sustained across transitions in leadership, that might not be the case in every district. New leadership either in the superintendent or the board can bring new priorities. Some leaders look to make their mark by moving away from the priorities of the prior superintendent and some boards feel that they were elected to make significant changes in direction. Circumstances and priorities in a district may also change dramatically based on economic or political developments.

Therefore, these case studies speak to the evolution of six districts' SEL programs through 2022 and the lessons we can learn from that evolution. It will be important to take another look at these districts in five to ten years to determine the degree of sustainability that their efforts have had over time and what further lessons we may learn as a result.

Meanwhile, it's important to affirm that each of the districts in this book has made a long-term commitment to SEL and has retained stability in its leadership and focus. Each of these districts is a demonstration of the possible. None is perfect and all remain works in progress. What sustains their commitment to SEL is their focus on a vision of school as a caring, inclusive, culturally responsive, and healthful place where children can grow to be successful in their own lives, as well as compassionate and responsible members of the community. And it is that vision, and the knowledge that the vision is indeed attainable, that makes this work so promising and inspiring.

References

Ablon, J. S. (2018). *Changeable: How collaborative problem solving changes lives at home, at school, and at work.* Penguin Random House.

Achor, S. (2012). *The orange frog: A parable based on positive psychology.* International Thought Leader Network.

Bardige, B. (1988). Things so finely human: Moral sensibilities at risk in adolescence. In C. Gilligan, J. V. Ward, J. M. Taylor, and B. Bardige (Eds.), *Mapping the moral domain* (pp. 87–110). Harvard University Press.

Barr, D. J., and Bardige, B. (2013). Case study 18A: Facing History and Ourselves. In P. M. Brown, M. W. Corriga, and A. Higgins-D'Alessandro (Eds.), *Handbook of prosocial education* (Vol. 2, pp. 665–680). Rowman & Littlefield.

Barr, D. J., Boulay, B., Selman, R. L., McCormick, R., Lowenstein, E., Gamse, B., Fine, M., and Leonard, M. B. (2015). A randomized controlled trial of professional development for interdisciplinary civic education: Impacts on humanities teachers and their students. *Teachers College Record, 117*(2), 1–52. doi: 10.1177/016146811511700202

Berg, J., Osher, D., Moroney, D., and Yoder, N. (2017, February). *The intersection of school climate and social and emotional development.* Washington, D.C.: American Institutes for Research. https://www.air.org/sites/default/files/2021-06/Intersection-School-Climate-and-Social-and-Emotional-Development-February-2017.pdf

Berman, S. (1997). *Children's social consciousness and the development of social responsibility.* State University of New York Press.

Berman, S. (2021). A path to equity paved by social-emotional learning. *School Administrator, 78*(7), 15–16.

Berman, S., Chaffee, S., and Sarmiento, J. (2018). *The practice base for how we learn: Supporting students' social, emotional, and academic development: Consensus statements of evidence from the Council of Distinguished Educators.* National Commission on Social, Emotional and Academic Development, The Aspen Institute. https://www.aspeninstitute

.org/publications/practice-base-learn-supporting-students-social-emotional-academic-development/

Berman, S., Chang, F., and Barnes, J. (2012). The district superintendent's role in supporting prosocial education. In A. Higgins-D'Alessandro, P. Brown, M. Corrigan, and B. W. Straub (Eds.), *The prosocial education handbook* (pp. 691–708). Rowman & Littlefield.

Berman, S., Jodl, J., and Barnes, J. (2023). The SEL roadmap: Avoiding the roadblocks, ruts, and dead ends. In S. E. Rimm-Kaufman, M. J. Strambler, and K. A. Schonert-Reichl (Eds.), *Social and emotional learning in action: Creating systemic change in schools* (pp. 211–234). Guilford Press.

Blewitt, C., Fuller-Tyszkiewicz, M., Nolan, A., Bergmeier, H., Vicary, D., Huang, T., McCabe, P., McKay,T., and Skouteris, H. (2018). Social and emotional learning associated with universal curriculum-based interventions in early childhood education and care centers: A systematic review and meta-analysis. *JAMA Network Open, 1*(8). doi: 10.1001/jamanetworkopen.2018.5727

Boncu, A., Costea, I., and Minulescu, M. (2017). A meta-analytic study investigating the efficiency of socio-emotional learning programs on the development of children and adolescents. *Romanian Journal of Applied Psychology, 19*(2), 35–41. doi: 10.24913/rjap.19.2.02

Brackett, M. A., Rivers, S. E., Reyes, M. R., and Salovey, P. (2012). Enhancing academic performance and social and emotional competence with the RULER feeling words curriculum. *Learning and Individual Differences, 22*(2), 218–224. doi: 10.1016/j.lindif.2010.10.002

CASEL. (2021, November 10). *2011–2021: 10 years of social and emotional learning in U.S. school districts: Elements for long-term sustainability of SEL*. https://casel.org/cdi-ten-year-report/

CASEL. (2022). *CASEL's district resource center*. https://drc.casel.org/

CASEL. (n.d.). *Fundamentals of SEL*. https://casel.org/fundamentals-of-sel/

Celio, C. I., Durlak, J. & Dymnicki, A. (2011). A meta-analysis of the impact of service-learning on students. *Journal of Experiential Education, 34*(2), 164–181. doi: 10.1177/105382591103400205

Center for the Collaborative Classroom. (2021). *Being a reader implementation handbook: Second edition*. https://www.collaborativeclassroom.org/programs/being-a-reader/

Cipriano, C., Strambler, M. J., Naples, L., Ha, C., Kirk, M. A., Wood, M. E., Sehgal, K et al. (2023). Stage 2 Report: The state of evidence for social and emotional learning: A contemporary meta-analysis of universal school-based SEL interventions. (Under review). *Child Development.* doi: 10.31219/osf.io/mk35u

Cleveland Metropolitan School District. (2024). *Cleveland teachers union contract, July 1, 2021–June 30, 2024*. https://www.clevelandmetroschools.org/

cms/lib/OH01915844/Centricity/Domain/160/Cleveland%20Teachers%20 Union%20Contract%202021-2024.pdf

Coburn, C. E. (2003). Rethinking scale: Moving beyond numbers to deep and lasting change. *Educational Researcher*, *32*(6), 3–12. doi: 10.3102 /0013189X032006003

Corcoran, R. P., Cheung, A. C. K., Kim, E., and Xie, C. (2018). Effective universal school-based social and emotional learning programs for improving academic achievement: A systemic review and meta-analysis of 50 years of research. *Educational Research Review*, *25* (November), 56–72. doi: 10 .1016/j.edurev.2017.12.001

Corvalllis School District. (2022, December 5). *2022–23 Student parent handbook*. https://www.csd509j.net/wp-content/uploads/2022-23-Student -Parent-Handbook-English.pdf

Darling-Hammond, L. F., Cook-Harvey, C., Barron, B., and Osher, D. (2020). Implications for educational practice of the science of learning and development. *Applied Developmental Science*, *24*(2), 97–140. doi: 10.1080 /10888691.2018.1537791

Domenech, D. A., Sherman, M., and Brown, J. L. (2022). *Leading social-emotional learning in districts and schools: A handbook for superintendents and other district leaders*. Rowman & Littlefield.

Domitrovich, C. E., Harris, A. R., Syvertsen, A. K., Morgan, N., Jacobson, L., Cleveland, M., Moore, J. E., and Greenberg, M. T. (2022). Promoting social and emotional learning in middle school: Intervention effects of Facing History and Ourselves. *Journal of Youth and Adolescence*, *51*(7), 1426–1441. doi: 10.1007/s10964-022-01596-3

Durlak, J. A., Weissberg, R. P., Dymnicki, A. B., Taylor, R. D., and Schellinger, K. B. (2011). The impact of enhancing students' social and emotional learning: A meta-analysis of school-based universal interventions. *Child Development*, *82*(1), 405–432. doi: 10.1111/j.1467-8624.2010.01564.x

Elias, M. J., Zins, J. E., Weissberg, R. P., Frey, K. S., Greenberg, M. T., Haynes, N. M., Kessler, R., Schwab-Stone, M. E., and Shriver, T. P. (1997). *Promoting social and emotional learning: Guidelines for educators*. Association for Supervision and Curriculum Development.

Faria, A-M., Kendziora, K., Brown, L., O'Brien, B., and Osher, D. (2013). *PATHS implementation and outcome study in the Cleveland Metropolitan School District: Final report*. American Institutes for Research. https: //www.air.org/resource/report/paths-implementation-and-outcome-study -cleveland-metropolitan-school-district-final

Fein, H. (1979). *Accounting for Genocide*. Free Press.

Goldberg, J. M., Sklad, M., Elfrink, T. R., Schreurs, K. M. G., Bohlmeijer, E. T., and Clarke, A. M. (2019). Effectiveness of interventions adopting a whole school approach to enhancing social and emotional development: A meta-analysis. *European Journal of Psychology of Education, 34*(4), 755–782. doi: 10.1007/s10212-018-0406-9

Greenberg, M. T. (2023). *Evidence for social and emotional learning in schools*. Learning Policy Institute. doi: 10.54300/928.269

Greenberg, M. T., Brown, J. L., and Abenavoli, R. M. (2016). *Teacher stress and health effects on teachers, students, and schools*. Edna Bennett Pierce Prevention Research Center, Pennsylvania State University, 1–12. https://prevention.psu.edu/publication/teacher-stress-and-health-effects-on-teachers-students-and-schools/

Greenberg, M. T., Weissberg, R. P., O'Brien, M. U., Zins, J. E., Fredericks, L., Resnik, H., and Elias, M. J. (2003). Enhancing school-based prevention and youth development through coordinated social, emotional, and academic learning. *American Psychologist, 58*(6–7), 466–474. doi: 10.1037/0003-066X.58.6-7.466

Hagelskamp, C., Brackett, M. A., Rivers, S. E., and Salovey, P. (2013). Improving classroom quality with the RULER approach to social and emotional learning: Proximal and distal outcomes. *American Journal of Community Psychology, 51*(3–4), 530–543. doi: 10.1007/s10464-013-9570-x

Heath, C., and Heath, D. (2017). *The power of moments*. Simon & Schuster.

Igoe, C., and Xagas, L. (2018). *One district's journey: From commitment to assessment*. CASEL. Retrieved April 2022 from https://measuringsel.casel.org/one-districts-journey-commitment-assessment/

Illinois State Board of Education. (2022). *Social emotional learning standards*. Retrieved April 2022 from https://www.isbe.net/Documents/SEL-Standards.pdf#search=SEL%20standards

Jackson, P. (1968). *Life in classrooms*. Holt, Rinehart, and Winston.

Jagers, R. J., Rivas-Drake, D., and Williams, B. (2019). Transformative social and emotional learning (SEL): Toward SEL in service of educational equity and excellence. *Educational Psychologist, 54*(3), 162–184. doi: 10.1080/00461520.2019.1623032

Jennings, P. A., and Greenberg, M. T. (2009). The prosocial classroom: Teacher social and emotional competence in relation to student and classroom outcomes. *Review of Educational Research, 79*(1), 491–525. doi: 10.3102/0034654308325693

Jones, S. M., Brush, K. E., Ramirez, T., Mao, Z. X., Marenus, M., Wettje, S., Finney, K., Raisch, N., Podoloff, N., Kahn, J., Barnes, S., Stickle, L., Brion-Meisels, G., McIntyre, J., Cuartas, J., and Bailey, R. (2021, July). *Navigating SEL from the inside out—Looking inside and across 33 leading SEL programs: A practical resource for schools and OST providers: Preschool and elementary focus*. 2nd ed. The EASEL Lab @ The Harvard

Graduate School of Education. https://www.wallacefoundation.org/knowledge-center/Documents/navigating-social-and-emotional-learning-from-the-inside-out-2ed.pdf

Jones, S. M., Brush, K. E., Wettje, S., Ramirez, T., Poddar, A., Kannarr, A., Barnes, S. P., Hooper, A., Brion-Meisels, G., and Chng, E. (2022, November). *Navigating SEL from the inside out—Looking inside and across leading SEL programs: A practical resource for schools and OST providers: Middle & high school focus.* The EASEL Lab @ The Harvard Graduate School of Education. https://www.wallacefoundation.org/knowledge-center/Documents/navigating-social-and-emotional-learning-from-the-inside-out-middle-high-school.pdf

Jones, S. M., and Kahn, J. (2017). *The evidence base for how we learn: Supporting students' social, emotional, and academic development—Consensus statements of evidence from the Council of Distinguished Scientists.* National Commission on Social, Emotional, and Academic Development, The Aspen Institute. https://www.aspeninstitute.org/publications/evidence-base-learn/

Kendziora, K., and Osher, D. (2016). Promoting children's and adolescents' social and emotional development: District adaptations of a theory of action. *Journal of Clinical Child and Adolescent Psychology, 45*(6), 797–811. doi: 10.1080/15374416.2016.1197834

Kendziora, K., and Yoder, N. (2016). *When districts support and integrate social and emotional learning (SEL): Findings from an ongoing evaluation of districtwide implementation of SEL.* Education Policy Center at American Institutes for Research. https://www.air.org/sites/default/files/2021-06/When-Districts-Support-and-Integrate-SEL-October-2016.pdf

Kusché, C. A., and Greenberg, M. T. (2011). The PATHS curriculum: Promoting emotional literacy, prosocial behavior, and caring classrooms. In S. Jimerson, A. Nickerson, M. J. Mayer, M. J. Furlong (Eds.) *Handbook of school violence and school safety: International research and practice,* 435–446. Routledge.

Learning Policy Institute & Turnaround for Children. (2021). *Design principles for schools: Putting the science of learning and development into action.* https://learningpolicyinstitute.org/sites/default/files/product-files/SoLD_Design_Principles_Principle_3_Rich_Learning.pdf

Lieberman, M. (1991). *Facing History and Ourselves: Evaluation report 1990.* Responsive Methodology.

Luo, L., Reichow, B., Snyder, P., Harrington, J., and Polignano, J. (2022). Systematic review and meta-analysis of classroom-wide social-emotional interventions for preschool children. *Topics in Early Childhood Special Education, 42*(1), 4–19. doi: 10.1177/0271121420935579

Lyon, A. R. (2017, July). *Implementation science and practice in the education sector: Brief prepared for Project AWARE grant recipients*. Substance Abuse and Mental Health Services Administration. https://education.uw.edu/sites/default/files/Implementation%20Science%20Issue%20Brief%20072617.pdf

Mahoney, J. L., Durlak, J. A., and Weissberg, R. P. (2018). An update on social and emotional learning outcome research. *Phi Delta Kappan, 100*(4), 18–23. doi: 10.1177/0031721718815668

Mertens, E. C. A., Deković, M., van Londen, M., Spitzer, J. E., and Reitz, E. (2022). Components related to long-term effects in the intra- and interpersonal domains: A meta-analysis of universal school-based interventions. *Clinical Child and Family Psychology Review*, 1–19. doi: 10.1007/s10567-022-00406-3

Moir, T. (2018). Why is implementation science important for intervention design and evaluation within educational settings? *Frontiers in Education, 3*, 61. doi: 10.3389/feduc.2018.00061

Murano, D., Sawyer, J. E., and Lipnevich, A. A. (2020). A meta-analytic review of preschool social and emotional learning interventions. *Review of Educational Research, 90*(2), 227–263. doi: 10.3102/0034654320914743

Naperville 203 Community School Unit. (n.d.a). *Diversity and inclusion*. Retrieved April 2022 from https://www.naperville203.org/Page/7176

Naperville 203 Community School Unit. (n.d.b) *Diversity and inclusion: Comprehensive equity plan*. Retrieved April 2022 from https://www.naperville203.org/Page/8171

Naperville 203 Community School Unit. (n.d.c). *Diversity and inclusion: Pillar 3: Equity centered schools and classroom practices*. Retrieved April 2022 from https://www.naperville203.org/Page/8657

Oliveira, S., Roberto, M. S., Pereira, N. S., Marques-Pinto, A., and Veiga-Simão, A. M. (2021). Impacts of social and emotional learning interventions for teachers on teachers' outcomes: A systematic review with meta-analysis. *Frontiers in Psychology, 12*. doi: 10.3389/fpsyg.2021.677217

Osher, D., Poirer, J. M., Dwyer, K. P., Hicks, R., Brown, L. J., Lampron, S., and Rodriguez, C. (2008). *Cleveland Metropolitan School District human ware audit: Findings and recommendations*. American Institutes for Research. https://www.air.org/sites/default/files/AIR_ClevelandHumanWareAudit_Report-2008.pdf

Osher, D., Poirer, J. M., Jarjoura, G. R., Haight, K., and Mitchell, D. (2014). *Follow-up assessment of conditions for learning in the Cleveland Metropolitan School District: Final report*. American Institutes for Research. https://www.air.org/project/cleveland-metropolitan-school-district-human-ware-initiative

Responsive Classroom. (n.d.) *Principles and practices.* https://www.responsiveclassroom.org/about/principles-practices/

Rimm-Kaufman, S. & Chiu, Y. (2007). Promoting social and academic competence in the classroom: An intervention study examining the contribution of the Responsive Classroom approach. *Psychology in the Schools, 44*(4), 397–413. doi: 10.1002/pits.20231

Rimm-Kaufman, S. E., Fan, X., Chiu, Y. J., & You, W. (2007). The contribution of the Responsive Classroom approach on children's academic achievement: Results from a three year longitudinal study. *Journal of School Psychology, 45*(4), 401–421. doi: 10.1016/j.jsp.2006.10.003

Rivers, S. E., Brackett, M. A., Reyes, M. R., Elbertson, N. A., and Salovey, P. (2013). Improving the social and emotional climate of classrooms: A clustered randomized controlled trial testing the RULER approach. *Prevention Science, 14*(1), 77–87. doi: 10.1007/s11121-012-0305-2

Schaps, E., Battistich, V., and Solomon, D. (2004). Community in school as key to student growth: Findings from the Child Development Project. In J. E. Zins, R. P. Weissberg, M. C. Wang, and H. J. Walberg (Eds.), *Building academic success on social and emotional learning: What does the research say?* (pp. 189–205). Teachers College Press.

Schultz, L. H., Barr, D. J., and Selman, R. L. (2001). The value of a developmental approach to evaluating character development programmes: An outcome study of Facing History and Ourselves. *Journal of Moral Education, 30*(1), 3–27. doi: 10.1080/03057240120033785

Schwartz, H. L., Bongard, E. D., Boyle, A. E., Meyers, D. C., and Jagers, R. J. (2022). Social and emotional learning in schools nationally and in the Collaborating Districts Initiative: Selected findings from the American Teacher Panel and American School Leader Panel surveys. Rand Corporation. doi: 10.7249/RRA1822-1

Sinek, Simon. (2009). *Start with why: How great leaders inspire everyone to take action.* Penguin.

Sklad, M., Diekstra, R., Ritter, M. D., Ben, J., and Gravesteijn, C. (2012). Effectiveness of school-based universal social, emotional, and behavioral programs: Do they enhance students' development in the area of skill, behavior, and adjustment? *Psychology in the Schools, 49*(9), 892–909. https://doi.org/10.1002/pits.21641

Solomon, D., Battistich, V., Watson, M., Schaps, E., and Lewis, C. (2000). A six-district study of educational change: Direct and mediated effects of the Child Development Project. *Social Psychology of Education, 4*, 3–51. doi: 10.1023/A:1009609606692

Solomon, D., Schaps, E., Watson, M., and Battistich, V. (1992). Creating caring school and classroom communities for all children. In R. Villa, J. Thousand, W. Stainback, and S. Stainback (Eds.), *Restructuring for caring and effective education: An administrative guide to creating heterogeneous schools* (pp. 41–60). Paul H. Brookes.

Statista Research Department. (2023, January 2). *U.S. unemployment rates for large metropolitan areas October 2022.* https://www.statista.com/statistics/227169/unemployment-rates-in-the-us-by-area/

Stone, D., Holland, K., Bartholow, B., Crosby, A., Davis, S., and Wilkins, N. (2017). *Preventing suicide: A technical package of policy, programs, and practices.* Centers for Disease Control and Prevention. doi: 10.15620/cdc.44275

Substance Abuse and Mental Health Services Administration. (2014). *SAMHSA's Concept of Trauma and Guidance for a Trauma-Informed Approach.* HHS Publication No. (SMA) 14–4884. https://store.samhsa.gov/sites/default/files/d7/priv/sma14-4884.pdf

Tabak, R. G., Khoong, E. C., Chambers, D. A., and Brownson, R. C. (2012). Bridging research and practice: Models for dissemination and implementation research. *American Journal of Preventive Medicine, 43*(3), 337–350. doi: 10.1016/j.amepre.2012.05.024

Taylor, R. D., Oberle, E., Durlak, J. A., and Weissberg, R. P. (2017). Promoting positive youth development through school-based social and emotional learning interventions: A meta-analysis of follow-up effects. *Child Development, 88*(4), 1156–1171. doi: 10.1111/cdev.12864

Tyson, O., Roberts, C. M., and Kane, R. (2009). Can implementation of a resilience program for primary school children enhance the mental health of teachers? *Australian Journal of Guidance and Counselling, 19*, 116–130. doi: 10.1375/ajgc.19.2.116

van de Sande, M. C. E., Fekkes, M., Kocken, P. L., Diekstra, R. F. W., Reis, R., and Gravesteijn, C. (2019). Do universal social and emotional learning programs for secondary school students enhance the competencies they address? A systematic review. *Psychology in the Schools, 56*(10), 1545–1567. doi: 10.1002/pits.22307

Wang, M. T., Degol, J. L., Amemiya, J., Parr, A., and Guo, J. (2020, September). Classroom climate and children's academic and psychological wellbeing: A systematic review and meta-analysis. *Developmental Review, 57.* doi: 10.1016/j.dr.2020.100912

Watson, M., Battistich, V., and Solomon, D. (1997). Enhancing students' social and ethical development in schools: An intervention program and its effects. *International Journal of Educational Research, 27*, 571–586. https://www.academia.edu/28252400/Enhancing_students_social_and_ethical_development_in_schools

Weissberg, R. P., Durlak, J. A., Domitrovich, C. E., and Gullotta, T. P. (2015). Social and emotional learning: Past, present and future. In J. A. Durlak, C. E. Domitrovich, R. P. Weissberg, and T. P. Gullotta (Eds.), *Handbook of social and emotional learning: Research and practice* (pp. 3–19). Guilford Press.

Wigelsworth, M., Lendrum, A., Oldfield, J., Scott, A., ten Bokkel, I., Tate, K., and Emery, C. (2016). The impact of trial stage, developer involvement and international transferability on universal social and emotional learning programme outcomes: A meta-analysis. *Cambridge Journal of Education, 46*, 347–376. doi: 10.1080/0305764X.2016.1195791

Wright, A., Lamont, A., Wandersman, A., Osher, D., and Gordon, E. (2016). Accountability and SEL programs: The Getting To Outcomes approach. In J. Durlak, C. Domitrovich, R. Weissberg, and T. Gullota (Eds.), *Handbook of Social and Emotional Learning: Research and Practice* (pp. 500–515). Guilford Press.

Wyman, P. A., Brown, C. H., LoMurray, M., Schmeelk-Cone, K., Petrova, M., Yu, Q., Walsh, E., Tu, X., and Wang, W. (2010). An outcome evaluation of the Sources of Strength suicide prevention program delivered by adolescent peer leaders in high schools. *American Journal of Public Health, 100*(9):1653–1661. https://ajph.aphapublications.org/doi/full/10.2105/AJPH.2009.190025

Yang, W., Datu, J. A. D., Lin, X., Lau. M. M., and Li, H. (2019). Can early childhood curriculum enhance social-emotional competence in low-income children? A meta-analysis of the educational effects. *Early Education and Development, 30*(1), 36–59. doi: 10.1080/10409289.2018.1539557

Yorio, P. L., & Ye, F. (2012). A meta-analysis on the effects of service-learning on the social, personal, and cognitive outcomes of learning. *Academy of management learning & education, 11*(1), 9-27. doi: 10.5465/amle.2010.0072

Zhang, Y., Cook, C., and Smith, B. (2021). Program evaluation report of the CharacterStrong middle/high school (grades 6–12) social emotional learning program. https://drive.google.com/file/d/1aw2F2YYnow1VhZNnx-9qwjYG6uq0nCKo/view

About the Author

Sheldon H. Berman, EdD, served as superintendent of four districts in three states—Hudson, Massachusetts; Jefferson County (Louisville), Kentucky; Eugene, Oregon; and Andover, Massachusetts—spanning twenty-eight school years. He provided leadership in state superintendent associations as well as in local and national education organizations. He served as Massachusetts Association of School Superintendents President, receiving the Massachusetts Superintendent of the Year Award in 2003 and AASA's Distinguished Service Award in 2022, in addition to lifetime achievement awards for social-emotional learning from CASEL and character education from Character.org.

In each of the four districts he led, Berman implemented systemic SEL programs, and he currently serves as AASA's Lead Superintendent for Social-Emotional Learning. He has authored numerous articles and books on SEL topics, including *Children's Social Consciousness and the Development of Social Responsibility* and *Promising Practices in Teaching Social Responsibility.* He was a member of the Council of Distinguished Educators of the National Commission on Social, Emotional, and Academic Development and was the primary author of the commission's SEL practice report.

In addition, Berman has contributed guidance on administrative ethics through a decade of *School Administrator* Ethical Educator columns and coauthored *The Ethical Educator: Pointers and Pitfalls for School Administrators.* Over the course of his career, he has published a continuing stream of book chapters, articles, policy reports, and op-eds on timely issues, and has been an invited presenter at national and international gatherings on education-related issues and innovations.

www.ingramcontent.com/pod-product-compliance
Lightning Source LLC
Chambersburg PA
CBHW032046300426
44117CB00009B/1210